WHO IS DRACULA'S FATHER?

WHO IS DRACULA'S FATHER?

And Other Puzzles in Bram Stoker's Gothic Masterpiece

JOHN SUTHERLAND

ICON

First published in the UK in 2017
by Icon Books Ltd, Omnibus Business Centre,
39–41 North Road, London N7 9DP
email: info@iconbooks.com
www.iconbooks.com

This edition published in the UK in 2018 by Icon Books Ltd

Sold in the UK, Europe and Asia
by Faber & Faber Ltd, Bloomsbury House,
74–77 Great Russell Street,
London WC1B 3DA or their agents

Distributed in the UK, Europe and Asia
by Grantham Book Services,
Trent Road, Grantham NG31 7XQ

Distributed in the USA
by Publishers Group West,
1700 Fourth Street, Berkeley, CA 94710

Distributed in Australia and New Zealand
by Allen & Unwin Pty Ltd,
PO Box 8500, 83 Alexander Street,
Crows Nest, NSW 2065

Distributed in South Africa
by Jonathan Ball, Office B4, The District,
41 Sir Lowry Road, Woodstock 7925

Distributed in India by Penguin Books India,
7th Floor, Infinity Tower – C, DLF Cyber City,
Gurgaon 122002, Haryana

Distributed in Canada by Publishers Group Canada,
76 Stafford Street, Unit 300
Toronto, Ontario M6J 2S1

ISBN: 978-178578-407-1

Typeset in Photina MT by Marie Doherty

Printed and bound in Great Britain by Clays Ltd, Elcograf S.p.A.

For Paul Barber

ABOUT THE AUTHOR

John Sutherland is Lord Northcliffe Professor Emeritus at University College London and an eminent scholar in the field of Victorian fiction. He is the author of many works including *The Longman Companion to Victorian Fiction* (2009) and the bestselling popular titles *Is Heathcliff a Murderer?* (1996, reissued 2017) and *Can Jane Eyre be Happy?* (1997, reissued 2017). His more recent works include *The Brontësaurus* (2016) and *Frankenstein's Brain* (2018).

Contents

Preface

I believe the reward from reading fiction arises less from what you know than what you don't know – what, perhaps, you'll never know. Puzzles.

In what follows I have, as it were, picked up Bram Stoker's *Dracula* and shaken it, to see what puzzles fall out. Interspersed with those puzzles are a few separate features, including a brief biography of Stoker on page 14 and a short summary of *Dracula*'s narrative on page 99. Don't rely on the movie versions. They take liberties. (But enjoy the best of them. Even the worst sometimes afford a perverse pleasure. Who would not be charmed by *Dracula's Dog?*)

I was very lucky to be a friend of Dr Paul Barber in the 1980s, when I was working in America. Barber is the most admired of scholars who have looked, anthropologically, folklorically, and every which way at the vampire phenomenon. His conclusions are stated in his now classic work, *Vampires, Burial and Death* (1990, reprinted 2010). It's a masterly summation of fact, fiction and fantasy. And in the lighter-hearted cogitation, I have borne in mind Paul Barber's instruction that we should keep separate in our minds the 'folkloric vampire' and the 'fictional vampire'.

Lovers of *Dracula*, and those coming to it for the first time, are lucky to have the fullest critical biography yet produced:

David J. Skal's *Something in the Blood: The Untold Story of Bram Stoker, the Man Who Wrote Dracula* (2017). Insight into the novel has recently been further enriched by the facsimile reproduction and transcription of the author's preliminary memoranda in *Bram Stoker's Notes for Dracula*, edited by Robert Eighteen-Bisang and Elizabeth Miller (2008).

There is a wealth of discussion about *Dracula* on the web, upon which I have drawn. If I have missed any acknowledgement of what is borrowed, I apologise, and will make amends in future editions.

Judge of a man by his questions
rather than by his answers

VOLTAIRE

Who is Dracula's father?

༈

W ho spawned Dracula? There are two contenders worthy of discussion here. Elsewhere (see page 6) we will examine the popular notion that Dracula is none other than Vlad the Impaler, the infamous 15th-century prince of Wallachia – in which case his father would be Vlad II Dracul, a nobleman of similar rank. But there is another possibility.

Before he goes to Transylvania, Jonathan Harker bones up in the reading room of the British Museum. One can indulge a fanciful vision of him under Panizzi's great dome, alongside George Bernard Shaw.

We may note, in passing, that Bram Stoker actually started his five years of casual research for *Dracula* in the public library of Whitby, over a relaxing summer holiday in the town, in 1890. One book in particular caught his fancy, William Wilkinson's *An Account of the Principalities of Wallachia and Moldavia*. From that volume (there cannot have been an overwhelming demand for it in the library) Stoker took the following, transcribed, supposedly by Harker, verbatim into the narrative:

> In the population of Transylvania there are four distinct nationalities: Saxons in the South, and mixed

with them the Wallachs, who are the descendants of the Dacians; Magyars in the West, and Szekelys in the East and North. I am going among the latter, who claim to be descended from Attila and the Huns.

Later, in an outburst of genealogical bombast, Dracula, a distinguished member of Szekely nobility (who did not, incidentally, use the title 'count', but 'boyar'), makes the point that he did not originate among the lowly Hunnish rapers and pillagers, but from the loins of the great Hun himself:

'We Szekelys have a right to be proud, for in our veins flows the blood of many brave races who fought as the lion fights, for lordship. Here, in the whirlpool of European races, the Ugric tribe bore down from Iceland the fighting spirit which Thor and Wodin gave them, which their Berserkers displayed to such fell intent on the seaboards of Europe, ay, and of Asia and Africa too, till the peoples thought that the were-wolves themselves had come. Here, too, when they came, they found the Huns, whose warlike fury had swept the earth like a living flame, till the dying peoples held that in their veins ran the blood of those old witches, who, expelled from Scythia had mated with the devils in the desert. Fools, fools! What devil or what witch was ever so great as Attila, whose blood is in these veins?' He held up his arms.

Stoker made a note to himself that Dracula's first language is not Romanian. It is certified in the printed text, rather pedantically, when he informs the newly arrived lawyer: 'my friend Harker Jonathan – nay, pardon me. I fall into my country's habit of putting your patronymic first'. He means Hungarian. Hunnish.

Attila (406–453) qualifies as one of the cruellest world conquerors in history. The name remains well known and much referenced – as in Mrs Thatcher's nickname, 'Attila the Hen'. Once heard, never forgotten.

Attila preyed on the rubble of the Roman Empire earning himself the title 'The Scourge of God'. He approved the title, suggesting as it did that: (1) he was God's punitive instrument; (2) he could himself punish God, if the whim took him. He centred his evil empire in the land of the Hun, now called, in his memory, Hungary.

Dracula's claim, of course, may suggest only that he is Attila's distant descendant, but given that he has lived for many centuries, could he in fact be the direct offspring of the great Hun? Interesting in this respect is the unusually detailed (for the 5th century) account of the tyrant's death and funeral, as recorded at the time by the Roman historian Priscus of Panium. Attila died mysteriously, on his wedding night, still in his forties. God, doubtless, prepared a warm welcome for him. Jordanes (another Roman historian) summarises Priscus's account thus:

Shortly before he died ... [Attila] took in marriage a very beautiful girl named Ildico, after countless other wives, as was the custom of his race. He had given himself up to excessive joy at his wedding, and as he lay on his back, heavy with wine and sleep, a rush of superfluous blood, which would ordinarily have flowed from his nose, streamed in deadly course down his throat and killed him, since it was hindered in the usual passages ... On the following day, when a great part of the morning was spent, the royal attendants suspected some ill and, after a great uproar, broke in the doors. There they found the death of Attila accomplished by an effusion of blood, without any wound, and the girl with downcast face weeping beneath her veil. Then, as is the custom of that race, they plucked out the hair of their heads and made their faces hideous with deep wounds, that the renowned warrior might be mourned, not by effeminate wailings and tears, but by the blood of men.

His body lay in state for a statutory number of days. His army, frantic with grief, mourned by smearing their faces with blood, circling the silken burial tent on their horses. He was buried with huge pomp – but no one knows where. Legend has it a river was diverted to flow over his resting place, lest anyone find and despoil it. Millions of people had a bone to pick with Attila the Hun.

But was he really dead? Is Dracula Attila reincarnate – or even the still-alive Attila? Attila died by drinking his own blood. Is that what Dracula hints by holding up his arm in

Jonathan's face? Or, more likely, was Ildico, on that gory wedding night, impregnated? There is a Dan Brown novel lurking in that idea.

Attila, if we pursue this line of speculation, has waited all these centuries for what? To conquer not just a slice of eastern Europe, but the whole planet, man, woman and child. Now, in 1893, God's Scourge, in the (un)person of Count Dracula, is ready to strike. Beware humanity. Call on a talkative old Dutch professor: he may save us.

Is Count Dracula the great Impaler incarnate?

༺⚹༻

That Dracula is, more or less, the offspring of Attila is persuasive. There is, however, an alternative genealogy which has found greater favour with Dracula devotees. Namely, that Dracula is Vlad Tepes, later called the 'Impaler', (re)incarnate. If so, he has come down in the world over the centuries. Vlad Tepes was much more than a mere 'count', or 'boyar'. Vlad III (c. 1431–c. 1477) was, as Van Helsing labels him, a 'voivode' – a warrior prince of Wallachia.

Vlad Tepes has, in historical record, a double character. He was, and still is, memorialised as a hero who held back the Turks' Ottoman imperial tide. He was also, legend has it, a sadist of hideous ingenuity. It was something temperamental and, at the same time, astutely political. Only by a regime of terror could order be kept in his part of the world. It is a belief which eastern European rulers, from Turkey to Mongolia, have followed to Stalin and beyond.*

Vlad Tepes's cruelty was as theatrical as it was brutal. He is reported as coolly impaling 25,000 Turks while calmly

---

* See M.J. Trow, *Vlad the Impaler: In Search of the Real Impaler* (2003) and Radu Florescu and Raymond T. McNally, *Dracula, Prince of Many Faces* (1989).

eating his lunch on a table in front of the massacre with the screams of his victims as condiment to his meat. Lucky victims were merely spitted through the belly. Others met with more ingenious cruelties best not thought about. There is a painting recording the great Impaler nailing the turbans of a party of Turk envoys to their heads with nails – since they declined to remove their headgear in his august presence. He was, one concludes, a very witty sadist.

That the Count is the great Impaler reincarnate is the core of one of the most flamboyant (and hugely enjoyable) film treatments of the novel, *Bram Stoker's Dracula* (1992). The director, Francis Ford Coppola, bought the Impaler thesis wholesale, 25,000 and all.

The identification of Count Dracula, directly or indirectly, with Vlad the Impaler, is provably false. It arises from a cat's cradle of misapprehension originating in Van Helsing's passing comment: 'He [Dracula] must, indeed, have been that Voivode Dracula who won his name against the Turk, over the great river on the very frontier of Turkey-land' (an unhappy phrase; but the doctor is, himself, an incorrigible gobbler of the English language).

William Wilkinson's *An Account of the Principalities of Wallachia and Moldavia* (1820), which Stoker pored over in his 1890 summer holiday in Whitby (of which more later) was his trove for such details. Wilkinson notes that 'Dracula' in the Wallachian language means devil or dragon. But Wilkinson goes on to add that 'The Wallachians ... used to give this as a surname to any person who rendered himself conspicuous either by courage, cruel actions, or cunning'. (Vlad, as a name and title, originates with *vladeti*, meaning 'rule'. It is used widely. There are at least half a dozen Romanian footballers named 'Vlad', none reported to feed on blood.)

Many commentators have blithely assumed that Dracula and the great Impaler are one and the same or closely related. It is an irresistible temptation. But there is no warrant for it in the text of the novel. Had Stoker intended the connection it would surely have been signalled more obviously. It would have been too rich a detail not to dangle in front of the reader. The word 'impale' occurs nowhere in the text. Dracula does not impale. He osculates – the toothy 'kiss', not the sharp stick, is his weapon of choice.

Coppola's research team must have come up with the facts contradicting the Impaler thesis. But the fiction that Dracula was the great Impaler was too good not to be true. And, what the hell, it was only a movie.

How dead is Dracula?

༃

Two of the titles Stoker played with before hitting, late in the day, on *Dracula* were. 'The Un-Dead' and 'The Dead Un-Dead'.

Neither is as good as the single word which stands on the published page, oozing enigma for first readers (Place? Person? Thing?). But those dropped titles point to an interesting puzzle. It can be easily enough stated; it is less easily resolved:

1. Is Dracula dead – 'as a doornail', as the proverb puts it?

2. Is he dead but 'resurrected'? (There is plentiful anti-Christ symbolism in his depiction – did Stoker read Nietzsche?)

3. Is he immortal, or merely long-living, like Methuselah?

4. Was he, himself, vampirised?

5. Was he made, by recruitment and instruction, into what he now is by some Satanic super-vampire?

6. Does he represent an evolutionary leap by the human species?

7. Is he alien, extraterrestrial, not of this earth? In H.G. Wells's *The War of the Worlds*, published in the same summer 1897 month as *Dracula*, the Martians, we recall, are interplanetary blood-suckers.

I lean towards 5. The reason is a note scrawled in Stoker's early jottings for the novel. The Dracul/Dracula (father/son) family, he writes, 'had dealings with the Evil One. They learned his secrets in the Scholomance, amongst the mountains over Lake Hermanstadt, where the devil claims the tenth scholar as his due.'

Stoker derived this from one of his half-dozen principal sources, Emily Gerard's writings about 'Transylvanian Superstitions':

> As I am on the subject of thunderstorms, I may as well here mention the *Scholomance*, or school supposed to exist somewhere in the heart of the mountains, and where all the secrets of nature, the language of animals, and all imaginable magic spells and charms are taught by the devil in person. Only ten scholars are admitted at a time, and when the course of learning has expired and nine of them are released to return to their homes, the tenth scholar is detained by the devil as payment, and mounted upon an *Ismeju* (dragon) he becomes henceforward the devil's aide-de-camp, and assists him in 'making the weather', that is to say, preparing the thunderbolts.*

---

* Emily Gerard, 'Transylvanian Superstitions', *Nineteenth Century* (1885). Gerard repeated and elaborated on the subject in a number of subsequent publications. Stoker drew on her heavily.

Jason Colavito, to whom I'm indebted here, notes that 'Gerard's version of the story is not a professional one'. Colavito goes on to say that 'By luck, a folklorist, R.C. Maclagan, produced a report for the journal *Folklore* in 1897 that included a more accurate version of the story then-current in Transylvania'. Maclagan's report reads:

> Here we find that the *drac* is the devil in person, who instructs certain persons to be magicians and medicine men in a college under the earth. Of these, one in eight receives instruction during fourteen years, and on his return to earth he has the following power. By means of certain magical formulae he compels a dragon to ascend from the depths of a loch. He then throws a golden bridle with which he has been provided over his head, and rides aloft among the clouds, which he causes to freeze and thereby produces hail.*

The relevant element here is that Dracula half a millennium ago – the dark ages – was one of Satan's privileged adoptees. He signed a Faustian pact: his soul in exchange for superhuman knowledge and power (Dracula, one recalls, can create a microclimate wherever he goes).

This discussion can help us to make sense of a further puzzle in the last pages of the novel. Why does Dracula have a 'look of peace' on his face as he is killed? This is how his demise

---

* http://www.jasoncolavito.com/scholomance-the-devils-school.html

is described by Mina (the blood of Dracula is still in her veins, remember):

> I shall be glad as long as I live that even in that moment of final dissolution, there was in the face a look of peace, such as I never could have imagined might have rested there.

One would think having one's jugular ripped apart, and one's heart impaled on a bowie knife and one's castle reduced to rubble might be a trifle unpeaceful.

Along with Gerard – 'Madame Dracula', as she has been nicknamed – one of the acknowledged sources of *Dracula* was Henry Irving's starring performance as Mephisto in his 1885 hit version of *Faust* (a loose amalgam of Goethe and Marlowe). A much-quoted exchange from Marlowe finds the title character quizzing Mephisto about what damnation is:

> *Faust.* Where are you damn'd?
> *Meph.* In hell.
> *Faust.* How comes it then that thou art out of hell?
> *Meph.* Why, this is hell, nor am I out of it.

The whole corpus of modern 'absurd' drama pivots on that Marlovian observation: that hell is located within our human frame. It is not outside us, somewhere else. It is us, here: not a place but a condition. Samuel Beckett in ten words.

Why, to ask again, is Dracula's final expression, before he dissolves into wind-borne dust, one of 'peace'? Because he is, at long last, released from being Dracula. The contract he made on his graduation from the Scholasticon is terminated. He is free.

Bram Stoker (1847–1912), a short biography

Little of interest is to be found in the first 30 years of Bram Stoker's life. He was born the middle child of seven in Dublin. His father was a civil servant at the 'Castle' – the HQ of Irish colonial administration. Bram's birth coincided with the 'Great Hunger' and mass emigration from Ireland – themes which ingenious critics have woven into *Dracula*. The Stokers, though, were among the Protestant middle classes, for whom the potato was a side dish, and were insulated from the peasants' suffering.

Bram's father was twenty years older than his wife Charlotte, and it was she who sowed the seed of literature in her son. She had ample time to do so. Little 'Bram' (Abraham in full but nicknamed thus to distinguish him from his namesake father) was bedridden with a mysterious ailment for the first seven years of his life. Thereafter, he grew strong, shining at Trinity College, Dublin, in the debating hall, classroom, and on the sports field. On graduation, Bram followed his father into the Castle. His career there was rapid: by 1877 young Stoker had risen to the post of Inspector of Petty Sessions. Abraham Stoker Snr complacently noted that he could think of no young man who had risen so fast.

Photographs confirm Bram to have been strikingly handsome – the epitome of the manly 'red Irishman'. Two events transformed his life in 1878. He married the wispily beautiful Florence Balcombe in that year, winning her hand from a mortified Oscar Wilde. It may be that Bram had the more winning smile: his rival had what Florence saw as 'curly teeth'. The other event involved the theatre. From childhood, Bram had been stage-struck. Henry Irving's touring company played Dublin regularly in the mid-1870s. Stoker, a confirmed Irvingite, wrote an admiring review of the actor's Hamlet. It was well received. The young civil servant was summoned to Irving's suite at the Shelbourne where the two men talked until daybreak. The next evening, Stoker was informed that the great man had a 'special gift' for him. It turned out to be a recitation of Thomas Hood's melodramatic poem 'The Dream of Eugene Aram'. At the end of his performance, Irving tore off his necktie and collapsed in a swoon. 'The recitation was different, both in kind and degree, from anything I ever heard,' Stoker recalled. His own response he described as 'hysterical'.

Irving impulsively invited Stoker to be his 'stage manager'. Bram's father was horrified. Was there, commentators have wondered, physical seduction? Stoker was a confessed Whitmanite. On American theatrical tours, he made a point of throwing himself at the feet of the great poet. Whitman's 'inversion' was an open secret. We may ask but we shall never know: Stoker's private life is a locked cabinet.

One biographer, Daniel Farson, a remote descendant, plausibly deduces that after the birth of one child, Irving Noel, Florence withdrew conjugal access, protecting the Dresden-china looks which, even ten years later, led the *Punch* cartoonist George du Maurier to rank her as one of the three most beautiful women in London. Farson believes, as does the latest biographer, David J. Skal, that Stoker resorted to actresses and prostitutes and contracted syphilis – something that speculation can link with the infectious vampiric kiss.

The fact is, there is a tantalising blankness in the twenty years of Stoker's manly (but what kind of manly?) prime. Either the cabinet is empty, or, as a trained keeper of documents, he expertly covered his tracks. What does survive is the record of his efficient factotum service to Irving. The Lyceum would never have dominated the London theatrical world as it did without Stoker behind the scenes. As Irving's particular friend, Stoker dined and hobnobbed with the age's celebrities: Wilde (who forgave him Florence), Ellen Terry, James Abbott McNeill Whistler, Arthur Conan Doyle and Hall Caine (the beloved 'Hommy-Beg', to whom *Dracula* would be dedicated). And for six years in the 1890s, he worked and researched a work provisionally entitled 'The Un-Dead'. Eventually he came round to the Wallachian word for 'devil', *dracul*, thence *Dracula* (the '-a' suffix meaning 'son of').

Stoker boned up on Transylvania in the British Museum and while on holiday in Whitby. Other sources of the novel were nearer to hand, notably fellow Irishman Joseph Sheridan Le Fanu's *Carmilla* (1872). What Stoker brought to vampirology was the frisson of his 'master' Irving's hypnotic stage presence, most spectacularly displayed in his performance as Mephistopheles in *Faust*. George du Maurier's sinister Svengali, from his novel *Trilby*, is also there somewhere. Stoker himself nodded towards Jack the Ripper as a topical inspiration. The fact is, so opaque are *Dracula*'s symbolisms that one can read virtually anything into them – and critics have.

Two events combined to alter the course of Stoker's life in 1897. One was the completion of *Dracula*; the other the burning down of the Lyceum warehouse, with all the company's props and wardrobe. Irving refused to stage, or even read, the dramatic adaptation of *Dracula* which Stoker had prepared (for copyright reasons). He affected to think poorly of his protégé's novel. It was wounding. The novel was, in the event, not an overwhelming sales success and would not take off as an international bestseller until a succession of screen versions made it a gold mine – though not for Irving, nor for Stoker's widow, Florence, who survived Bram by 25 years, most of them tormented by *Dracula* copyright squabbles.

Stoker was no longer necessary to Irving after the Lyceum closed in 1902. The actor, disabled by a series of strokes, died three years later. Whether it was syphilis or not, Stoker's last ten years were difficult. He too suffered strokes and chronic poor health but nonetheless forced himself to turn out six 'shockers', none of them in the same class as *Dracula*. Everyone, it is said, has one novel inside them. Would they were all as good as Stoker's.

What colour is Dracula's moustache?

⤜⤛

It depends when and where you look at him. The driver who picks up Jonathan Harker on the eve of Saint George's Day – when wolves go crazy and the earth combusts randomly into blue flame – is not immediately identified.

But Dracula has no servants or household staff (an interesting detail – see 'Who Washes Dracula's Pinafore?', page 37). No stable hands, grooms, or muckers-out. It is hard to picture the master doing it, but do it somebody must.

The whip-lashing driver who hurries Jonathan Harker off to his doom in a hearse-like vehicle, drawn by four black horses, possesses 'prodigious' strength. Wolves cringe and whimper in his presence. We can, from the first, make a good guess at whom the alpha wolfish driver must be. Harker later confirms it was the Count himself. This is how the (un)man is described by Harker, in his diary:

> They [his four black horses] were driven by a tall man, with a long brown beard and a great black hat, which seemed to hide his face from us. I could only see the gleam of a pair of very bright eyes, which seemed red in the lamplight, as he turned to us.

NB the long brown beard.

The extravagantly hirsute driver speaks no English, but excellent German. The coach goes round and round: killing time, we apprehend, until midnight on the Eve of St George, when Dracula (midnights and middays are good for him) draws a sustaining lease of undeadly strength.

When they finally arrive at Castle Dracula Harker is kept waiting outside forever in the cold (Dracula has welcomed his guest with a microclimate of early summer snow). Stable business, one supposes, is detaining his host. Finally the door, after much unbolting and creaking, swings open on its century-old rusty hinges and:

> Within, stood a tall old man, clean shaven save for a long white moustache, and clad in black from head to foot, without a single speck of colour about him anywhere. He held in his hand an antique silver lamp, in which the flame burned without chimney or globe of any kind, throwing long quivering shadows as it flickered in the draught of the open door.

He now speaks 'excellent' English. And he must, after stabling the horses, have been busy with the razor and the hair dye.

No beard. And his moustache is now white. There are various references by witnesses in the course of the novel describing Dracula which confirm an occasionally white moustache and thin beard streaked with white. The labourer who humped his large, earth-filled boxes on their way to Carfax recalls that:

'There was the old party what engaged me a-waitin' in the 'ouse at Purfleet. He 'elped me to lift the boxes and put them in the dray. Curse me, but he was the strongest chap I ever struck, an' him a old feller with a white moustache, one that thin you would think he couldn't throw a shadder.'

Nor can any vampire, as it happens, cast a 'shadder'.

On another occasion, a terrified Jonathan and mystified Jack catch sight of the count, incognito, in London, sporting radically different facial hair:

[Jonathan] was very pale, and his eyes seemed bulging out as, half in terror and half in amazement, he gazed at a tall, thin man, with a beaky nose and black moustache and pointed beard, who was also observing the pretty girl. He was looking at her so hard that he did not see either of us, and so I had a good view of him. His face was not a good face; it was hard, and cruel, and sensual, and his big white teeth that looked all the whiter because his lips were so red, were pointed like an animal's. Jonathan kept staring at him, till I was afraid he would notice. I feared he might take it ill, he looked so fierce and nasty. I asked Jonathan why he was disturbed, and he answered, evidently thinking that I knew as much about it as he did: 'Do you see who it is?'

He is now facially embellished with a black moustache and goatee.

In the most blood-curdling image of him, in one of his boxes, there is yet another mutation of facial hair:

I knew I must reach the body for the key, so I raised the lid, and laid it back against the wall; and then I saw something which filled my very soul with horror. There lay the Count, but looking as if his youth had been half renewed, for the white hair and moustache were changed to dark iron-grey; the cheeks were fuller, and the white skin seemed ruby-red underneath; the mouth was redder than ever, for on the lips were gouts of fresh blood, which trickled from the corners of the mouth and ran over the chin and neck. Even the deep, burning eyes seemed set amongst swollen flesh, for the lids and pouches underneath were bloated. It seemed as if the whole awful creature were simply gorged with blood. He lay like a filthy leech, exhausted with his repletion.

A very hirsute leech – a species unknown outside Transylvania, one suspects.

So, to chart the changes – the novel's pogonotrophy, to use the biggest word available to moustache scholarship – we have Dracula with enough brown beard and moustache to stuff a pillow; a Dracula with a white moustache and thin beard, sometimes white-streaked: a Dracula with a pitch-black moustache and goatee; a Dracula clean-shaven but for an iron-grey Hindenburg moustache; and some variations of the above.

Clearly Dracula's intake of blood has something to do with the profusion, hue and age-fade of his facial hair. But the ease with which his ancient, scrawny, white-haired self can lift huge boxes with the ease of a Schwarzenegger suggests it is not the whole story.

The truth – which requires a long stretch of the imagination – is that Dracula has no physical existence whatsoever. In a note Stoker recorded that his weight was a few ounces. Hence he throws no shadow and has no mirror image. There is nothing there to reflect. He can be a bat, a rat, a wolf, a mist, or a Romanian aristocrat. All without solidity. He is a shape-changer at will. And his moustache too is an ever-mutating detail.

It is not easy to transfer this literally *dissolute* condition to the screen. Bela Lugosi's chin, we recall, is as hairless as a snooker ball and meaty enough to advertise the 1930s Gillette blue razor. Lugosi's Dracula is physical. Gary Oldman is clean shaven, but amazingly coiffed in his homely castle (where he has nothing to do by day, over the many centuries, but fuss with his hair). He is modishly hairy on the London streets. In Piccadilly he looks like just another dandy. One could go on. It remains not a puzzle, but a source of puzzles. And, like so many things in this inexhaustible novel, the more you explore, the more puzzling it becomes.

Quincey P. Morris: vampire?

꙳

W ho is Quincey P. Morris? He pops up in the narrative like a genie from a bottle. One rub, and Quincey P. is suddenly there. Ready to serve. How and where it was he fell in love with Lucy Westenra, and she not quite in love with Quincey P. Morris, lies never to be known in the dark hinterland of the un-narrated.

The kind of outdoorsy fellow he is would have been readily recognisable to any wide-awake 1890s reader. Buffalo Bill [Cody] was, in the 1890s, a Yank much better known in England than whoever the current US President was in 1895 (Grover S. Cleveland – which probably doesn't tell the average reader much).

Quincey P. Morris is, manifestly, inspired by Buffalo Bill. The legendary showman cowboy, with his 'Wild West Show', made a sensational first visit to the UK in 1887, entrancing the population with his exploits with horse, lasso, and six-shooter. Britain was crazy for Bill's Wild West Show. Victoria ordered a 'command performance' at Windsor Castle. We were amused.*

Bram Stoker and Henry Irving were pals with Cody at the

....
* See Louis S. Warren's informative article (available online), 'Buffalo Bill meets Dracula: William F. Cody, Bram Stoker and the Frontiers of Racial Decay'.

time of his 1887 English tour, having first met him on Irving's own US tours. Immortalised in dime novels, one can imagine Cody reading *Dracula* by the old fire, having had his evening chow (buffalo fritters).

As Stoker portrays him Quincey is a buck-skinned Texan, formidably armed. He carries a rhino-handled bowie knife (named after the legendary knife-fighter, Jim Bowie, who died at the Alamo, taking a goodly number of Mexicans with him). In his notes for the novel Stoker equipped Brutus M. Marix, as Quincey was originally called, with a Maxim machine gun. In the published text, a repeater-action Winchester rifle was preferred. Doubtless Quincey has a couple of handier miniature derringers stashed in his high boots.*

A big-game hunter who has slaughtered innocent wildlife across the globe from frozen Siberia to the scorching tropics, Quincey is vastly rich. There is in him more than a touch of Teddy Roosevelt, the only American President to have shot five African elephants and called the 'cowboy candidate'.

Quincey and his inseparable buddy 'Art' (i.e. Arthur, Lord Holmwood) have hunted and slept under canvas together in wild places. It's the kind of thing which bonds men.

As Quincey reminisces about their transatlantic friendship:

....
* Stoker made further use of the cowboy stereotype with Grizzly Dick (an unhappy name) in his short story *The Shoulder of Shasta* (1895).

We've told yarns by the camp-fire in the prairies; and dressed one another's wounds after trying a landing at the Marquesas; and drunk healths on the shore of Titicaca.

As Wikipedia* informs us, 'Lake Titicaca is a large, deep lake in the Andes on the border of Peru and Bolivia. By volume of water and by surface area, it is the largest lake in South America.' Nothing small for Quincey P. Morris. The blood connection ('dressed one another's wounds') between Art and Quince is, I suggest, worth noting.

Under his cowboy guise Quincey P. Morris is a highly civilised WASP (as was Theodore Roosevelt Jr) but, for English people, he plays up to their cretinous image of the homespun, rootin', tootin', tobacco-chewin', gun-totin' American. As Lucy says:

Mr. Morris doesn't always speak slang – that is to say, he never does so to strangers or before them, for he is really well educated and has exquisite manners – but he found out that it amused me to hear him talk American slang, and whenever I was present, and there was no one to be shocked, he said such funny things.

His proposal of marriage to her is appropriately slangy:

....

* Accessed June 2017.

'Won't you just hitch up alongside of me and let us go down the long road together, driving in double harness?'

A 'Yippee-ai-eh!' would have been in order, had the young gal given him the old 'yessiree'. She did not.

One registers the fact that Quincey is deuced clever at pretending to be what, manifestly, he is not. Some have been inspired to speculate whether Mr Morris is in fact an inductee into Dracula's army of the un-dead. The idea has been played with by various writers in various ways. Perhaps Quincey has been recruited into the deadly crew before appearing on the novel's scene (Franco Moretti's theory, discussed below). Another angle is whether Quincey might rise after killing the Count – his master – as Dracula redivivus (as in P.N. Elrod's series of stories beginning with 'The Wind Breathes Cold'). Let's examine the charge sheet.

Significantly he's the last man to have intimate contact with Lucy. He donates his 'manly' blood. Little good it does. But his bodily fluid is inside Lucy on the last morning of her (live) life.

Then there is Quincey's inexplicable behaviour after Mina, in her turn, is found sucked dry by Dracula. Here is Seward recording events in his diary:

I raised the blind, and looked out of the window. There was much moonshine; and as I looked I could see Quincey Morris run across the lawn and hide himself in the shadow of a great yew-tree. *It puzzled me to think why he was doing this* ... [my emphasis]

When questioned, Quincey gives the following version of events:

'... I thought it well to know if possible where the Count would go when he left the house. I did not see him; but I saw a bat rise from Renfield's window, and flap westward. I expected to see him in some shape go back to Carfax; but he evidently sought some other lair. He will not be back to-night; for the sky is reddening in the east, and the dawn is close. We must work to-morrow!'

Even after she has turned him down and been betrothed to another, Quincey remains the most faithful of Lucy's suitors – to the death, literally. His death. But the description of his killing the Count, and himself dying, is, like much about Quincey P. Morris, foggy. Night is fast falling, whereupon Dracula will be invincible. Jonathan and Quincey fight their way through the knife-wielding gypsies (why, incidentally, are these men willing to die for Dracula, a corpse in a box?). Quincey receives a deadly wound, but is still able to fight his way to the Count's body. He goes for the heart, Jonathan for the head. Dracula, as night falls, dissolves into dust. Oddly, as noted above, he has a 'look of peace' in his eyes.

It all adds up crookedly. Franco Moretti in his influential

monograph, *Signs Taken for Wonders* (1983) indicts Quincey as Dracula's secret vampire ally:

> Lucy dies – and then turns into a vampire – immediately after receiving a blood transfusion from Morris. Nobody suspects ... [when] Morris leaves the room to take a shot – missing naturally – at the big bat ... or when, after Dracula bursts into the household Morris hides among the trees ... loses sight of Dracula and invites the others to call off the hunt for the night.

Add to Moretti's charge sheet the fact that through incompetence (or guile?) it is Quincey who allows Dracula to slip through his fingers and escape from London. Quincey actually uses the word 'vampire' before Van Helsing or any of the others in the England-based strand of the novel. He admits to personal acquaintance with the blood-suckers. His horse was fatally bitten, he recalls, when hunting on the Argentinian pampas, by a vampire bat (was Quincey also bitten?).

The evidence mounts up to something strange. Is there an American community of vampires? A cult, like the Mormons of Utah? Has Quincey been bitten by Dracula (where?) and 'turned'? Is he an ally of the Count? Rather subtly, Moretti sees a turncoat: 'So long as things go well for Dracula, Morris acts like an accomplice. As soon as there is a reversal of fortunes, he turns into his [Dracula's] staunchest enemy.'

I love curiosities. It is the reason for this book's being. But Stoker, for all his virtues, is not the lightest-fingered of narrators. Subtlety is not Bram Stoker's long suit. Had he meant us to suspect Quincey of double-dealing, he would have given us something more solid to chew on. A hint, at least. But novelists, as they write, may well keep something, a potential narrative twist, in reserve. Stoker may have thought he might want, as the novel went along, to complicate his characterisation of the Texan. In long-running TV serials (like *The Wire*, which had many such) they are called 'pipes'. Plot twists held *in potentia* should they be needed. I suspect Stoker may have been laying pipes with Quincey and, in the event, did not use them.

Where did Dracula's (English-speaking?) harem come from?

꽁꽁

Lucy Westenra receives three proposals of marriage all at once, as she confides, bubblingly, to her bosom friend Mina:

> Here am I, who shall be twenty in September, and yet I never had a proposal till to-day, not a real proposal, and to-day I have had three. Just fancy! THREE proposals in one day! Isn't it awful! I feel sorry, really and truly sorry, for two of the poor fellows. Oh, Mina, I am so happy that I don't know what to do with myself. And three proposals!

Oh, she wonders, if only the Law, and Holy Writ allowed 'triolism' (not Lucy's actual word; but what she means):

> Why can't they let a girl marry three men, or as many as want her, and save all this trouble? But this is heresy, and I must not say it.

In the novel as it plays out, Lucy is a demure maiden by day – a veritable Lady of Shallot – but a sexual predator by night, with an infected whore's charms ('Kiss me, Arthur [and die]'). If stenographic Mina represents the 'New Woman' of the 1890s, Lucy represents the *ewig weibliche*, the *femme fatale*, *la belle dame sans merci*, Jezebel.

Lucy's would-be husbands are an impressively husky crew: a lunatic asylum manager ('the mad doctor', as Stoker bluntly calls him in his notes), an ermined peer of the realm, and a gun-toting Texan millionaire. What 'heretical' romps the threesome could have in Lord Holmwood's castle.

They are already on the first step of conjugality. Arthur and Quincey have slept together, by the lapping shores of Lake Titiaca and body to body under fur in the snows of Siberia. Seward uses his doctor's privilege of examining Lucy's naked body, after night-time violation by her fourth lover, the bat Dracula.

Dracula is similarly inclined towards triolism. Unlike Lucy, he does not give a fig about 'heresy'. The count warms his coffined nights with three beautiful vampirettes (let's call them). In the novel they are called 'weird sisters' – alluding to the unlovely witches in *Macbeth*. It is not clear, given their colouring, that they are indeed siblings. Two have Dracula's 'aquiline' nose. It has led to speculation – unfounded – that they are his daughters. They are more often referred to as the 'brides of Dracula'. Two have raven-dark hair. The third is fair.

The sisters are routinely pictured voluptuously on screen by film-makers from Tod Browning onwards, making no secret of their carnal appeal to the male audience – dead or undead. Browning had them dressed in something between peignoir and wedding gown. Clad for action. Hammer films dispensed with wardrobe and went totally Playboy.

The scene in the novel in which the vampirettes are introduced has points of interest. Jonathan, despite the Count's stern prohibition, is exploring Castle Dracula by night. Echoes of Bluebeard's wife are recalled in the reader's mind. Jonathan comes on a room occupied by 'three young women, ladies by their dress and manner' (NB 'ladies', not lowly wenches).

They throw, he notes, no shadow on the floor, indicating they are fully 'turned'. They have supped Dracula's precious bodily fluids and he theirs. The Draculian sacrament. Jonathan's description of the trio is given in Stoker's high florid style:

All three had brilliant white teeth that shone like pearls against the ruby of their voluptuous lips. There was something about them that made me uneasy, some longing and at the same time some deadly fear. I felt in my heart a wicked, burning desire that they would kiss me with those red lips. It is not good to note this down, lest some day it should meet Mina's eyes and cause her pain; but it is the truth. They whispered together, and then they all three laughed – such a silvery, musical laugh, but as hard as though the sound never could have come through the softness of human lips. It was like the intolerable, tingling sweetness of water-glasses when played on by a cunning hand.

The fair girl shook her head coquettishly, and the other two urged her on. One said: –

'Go on! You are first, and we shall follow; yours is the right to begin.'

What 'right', one wonders, does she have? I have puzzled myself about this. She is the oldest sister, is the best I can come up with. Or that she is Dracula's favourite. His wife of the week, perhaps.*

Harker is at this moment both limp-limbed and erect with desire: 'I closed my eyes in a languorous ecstasy and waited – waited with beating heart.' He longs for the ravishing to come from these merciless *belles dames*. One two three. A vampiric triolistic orgy. No thought of virginal Mina, faithfully preserving herself in Whitby, banging away at her qwerty typewriter lessons.

Enter, at the very coital moment, the Count. In a fury. He beats the vampirettes back with the air of a husband who has discovered his wife misconducting herself with the untrousered postman:

'How dare you touch him, any of you? How dare you cast eyes on him when I had forbidden it? Back, I tell you all! This man belongs to me! Beware how you meddle with him, or you'll have to deal with me.'

---

* See also the note on 'Tresses', page 138.

Having denied them Jonathan, he throws his harem a live, 'half-smothered' baby which they devour gluttonously. A mere snack in a sack. Jonathan is detumescent with disgust at how near he came to something unspeakable. It may just be a stay of execution. After he has departed for England, the Count says, the sisters can feast on Jonathan:

> 'Back, back, to your own place! Your time is not yet come. Wait! Have patience! To-night is mine. To-morrow night is yours!' There was a low, sweet ripple of laughter, and in a rage I threw open the door, and saw without the three terrible women licking their lips. As I appeared they all joined in a horrible laugh, and ran away.

They live, undead, in the far background of the plot, waiting to be destroyed by Van Helsing's merciless hammer and stake. A death so phallic one need not even mention the symbology (to borrow that useful, nonsensical term from Dan Brown).

There is a teasing puzzle in this superheated orgiastic scene. What language are Dracula and his harem speaking in? Certainly not the local Romanian, nor the Hungarian that I have argued is the Count's native tongue, or else Jonathan would not have the faintest idea of what is being said. Possibly German; it depends on how bare a 'smattering' Harker in fact has (see 'How much German does Jonathan speak?', page 69). But there is another, more intriguing possibility: Dracula and these women are speaking fluent idiomatic English.

In which case we must deduce that they are English 'ladies'. How, though, did they end up in the coffined vaults of Castle Dracula? Or Transylvania, come to that. One needs to invent a narrative to answer the question at all plausibly. They were, let us fantasise, tourists – passengers, perhaps, of Mr Thomas Cook. Their 'aquiline' (eagle-like), Roman noses, like the Count's, indicate high birth. Alas, the ladies got lost in the woods (is the place not named 'Transylvania'*?). Dracula offered them (dangerous) refuge in his castle. The inevitable happened. He keeps the trio close for other things than their nutritive blood. As every adaptor of the original tale for the screen makes clear, Dracula has sexual appetites – or, as the sexologists nowadays coyly put it, 'interests'. The Devil (one of his putative fathers) is very interested in sex. As Thomas Aquinas, no less, wrote in *De Trinitate*:

> Devils do indeed collect human semen, by means of which they are able to produce bodily effects; but this cannot be done without some local movement, therefore devils can transfer the semen which they have collected and inject it into the bodies of others.

The image of Dracula collecting male semen by mouth is not something one wants to follow too far. But perhaps that is one reason he is holding Jonathan – not for his neck but elsewhere.

....
* It means 'beyond the woods'. Lovely name.

To go a little way down that route, witches testify that the devil has no scrotum or testicle but a penis whose characteristics he borrows from the goat. Along with the goat's notoriously insatiable appetites.

One of the problems, discussed elsewhere in this book (see page 61), is why Dracula takes the risk of coming to England. One answer lies in his vaults. He keeps no wine there, but receptacles of the English female blood he has developed a taste for. What's his score, as narrated in the novel? Lucy, her mother (possibly), Mina, the trio in the vaults. He does not bother with Renfield (who desperately wants to be bothered with). What do his harem have in common? They are 'ladies'.

Lock up your daughters England! And men, keep your flies zipped.

Who washes Dracula's pinafore?

✵

Dracula has been pictured on screen innumerable times, traditionally in full, immaculately pressed evening dress and cloak. Never, I would hazard, in a 'pinny', or soiled housemaid's apron. Nor, in any of the filmic depictions of *Dracula*, has the Count been shown doing the dishes, dusting, or – God help us – rinsing his underthings after a hard night out with the werewolves. Who brushes the coffin dirt off his shoulders? Who grooms his magnificent team of horses? Who cooks the food Jonathan Harker eats with relish?

Harker makes the point, several times, that his host has no servants. None whatsoever. Dracula himself, in disguise, is obliged to drive the carriage which brings the solicitor's clerk to the ominous castle (the delay in his opening the front door is explained, as I suggest above, by his having to unharness the horses in the stables behind the castle).

Dracula can, of course, transmute himself into bat, wolf, rat, dog or fog. But a housewife? Relevant here is Harker's undignified but informative keyhole peeping:

> I heard the great door below shut, and knew that the
> Count had returned. He did not come at once into
> the library, so I went cautiously to my own room and

found him making the bed. This was odd, but only confirmed what I had all along thought – that there were no servants in the house. When later I saw him through the chink of the hinges of the door laying the table in the dining-room, I was assured of it; for if he does himself all these menial offices, surely it is proof that there is no one else to do them. This gave me a fright, for if there is no one else in the castle, it must have been the Count himself who was the driver of the coach that brought me here.

A four-horse, whip-wielding carriage driver is one thing. Housemaid and washer-up (albeit of 600-year-old gold plate) something quite else. Let us prefer not to think about it. Stoker's notes indicate that when the Count is in England it was intended he should be helped in 'menial offices' by a couple of mute servants. One male, one female. They were dropped in the printed version. But the question of who is doing the washing up etc. at Castle Dracula remains to trouble the mind's eye. As does that brief, but unsettling, image of the master making beds, and presumably washing the bed sheets.

So who washes Dracula's apron? Dracula.

Why does Van Helsing swear in German?

꙳

On 9 September Seward records in his diary visiting Lucy, with Abraham Van Helsing, in her invalid bed. Deathbed it will soon be, they both sense. It is a direful visit

> As I raised the blind, and the morning sunlight flooded the room, I heard the Professor's low hiss of inspiration, and knowing its rarity, a deadly fear shot through my heart. As I passed over he moved back, and his exclamation of horror, 'Gott in Himmel!' needed no enforcement from his agonised face. He raised his hand and pointed to the bed, and his iron face was drawn and ashen white. I felt my knees begin to tremble.

Van Helsing's spontaneous ejaculation is strange. He's a Dutchman. It should be 'God in de hemel'. It doesn't roll off the tongue, but that, linguistically, is what it should be.

It's a puzzle. An answer is at hand. The reason for Van Helsing's erupting into German at moments of stress can be traced back to the literary origins of the omniscient, irrepressibly garrulous doctor in Stoker's first thinking about the novel.

In his early notes for Chapter 6 (written, probably, in 1890 or shortly after) Stoker notes the arrival of 'a German professor'. He initially had the *echt* German name of Professor Dr Max von Windshoeffel.*

Why, though, did Stoker later change the professor's nationality? And why need a German (or Dutch) know-all to come to the rescue? Are there not wise men enough at Oxford? The most convincing explanation throws a revealing light on *Dracula*'s inspirations and Stoker's later precautions lest those inspirations appear too obvious.

He knew, and certainly relished, the ghost stories of his fellow Dubliner, Sheridan Le Fanu, the acknowledged Victorian master of the genre, until, some would say, M.R. James came along.† Le Fanu's vampire tale *Carmilla* – often reckoned the greatest of its kind in the 19th century – was a seminal influence on *Dracula*. Stoker's book can be seen as not borrowing but homage.

A physically slighter work than Stoker's, *Carmilla* explores the lesbian possibilities of vampiric relationship. Stoker, as his notes testify, first thought to set *Dracula*, like *Carmilla*, in German-speaking Styria (now Austria), until, after coming on Emily Gerard, he had the bright idea of using Transylvania.

....

* Christopher Frayling, in *Vampyres: Lord Byron to Count Byron* (1992), makes the persuasive suggestion that Van Helsing is based on Professor Max Müller, the famous German scholar resident in England.
† James himself wrote a fine vampire tale, 'Count Magnus' (1904).

He was also probably motivated by the desire to put distance between himself and Le Fanu. Homage can quickly become plagiarism.

It is not *Carmilla* which entirely explains Van Helsing's odd teutonic outburst in Van Helsing. *Carmilla* was first published with other Le Fanu stories under the collective title *In a Glass Darkly*, supposedly all from the casebook of Dr Hesselius, a German practitioner of 'metaphysical medicine' – an occultist with a doctor's bag. In the short work 'Green Tea' Hesselius is more fully described. The hero-narrator offers a CV of this formidably omniscient scholar:

> In my wanderings I became acquainted with Dr. Martin Hesselius, a wanderer like myself, like me a physician, and like me an enthusiast in his profession. Unlike me in this, that his wanderings were voluntary, and he a man, if not of fortune, as we estimate fortune in England, at least in what our forefathers used to term 'easy circumstances'. He was an old man when I first saw him; nearly five-and-thirty years my senior.
>
> In Dr. Martin Hesselius, I found my master. His knowledge was immense, his grasp of a case was an intuition. He was the very man to inspire a young enthusiast, like me, with awe and delight. My admiration has stood the test of time and survived the separation of death. I am sure it was well-founded.

A string of cases Hesselius has solved are reeled off. We are further informed that Hesselius has a close friend, learned, like him, in very strange places – places that science dare not go. This friend is Dutch, Professor Van Loo of Leyden.

The Dutch professor is not, Like Dr Hesselius and the narrator, a physician (primarily) but a theoretical chemist and a man who has an expert grasp of history, metaphysics and biology. A little bit of everything. Hesselius corresponds with Van Loo in English and French but mainly German.

Stoker seeded Van Helsing's portrait with details not found in Le Fanu, all parenthetic, all poignant, none dwelt on. Van Helsing is aged, he is married, his son died, his wife went mad. Catholicism means he cannot divorce her. He doubts his faith and may even hate God. It is an understatedly tragic life whose defeats he can now redeem by defeating the arch-enemy of man. With hammer and stake in hand. His last words (the last words of the novel) resonate: 'We want no proofs; we ask none to believe us!' To have done it is enough. Van Helsing's great victory will be private.

Bram Stoker initially thought to create a German Hesselius semblance – Windshoeffel – then decided not to make it too obvious and to give it, fleetingly, unusual depths. Van Loo the Dutchman was a handy alternative. Hence Van Helsing.

Alle verstanden gnädige professoren.

J.S. Le Fanu's *Carmilla* (1872)

J.S. Le Fanu's pioneer vampire story, published in 1872, is set in Styria, where motherless Laura (who tells most of the story) has been brought up in the stately, empty castle owned by her English father. Not an everyday upbringing. Laura is prey to dreams in which her neck is punctured by a beautiful (female) lover. Her loneliness is relieved by the arrival of the captivating Carmilla, who mysteriously resembles Laura's dream lover. The physical relationship which ensues is described in the most overtly lesbian terms to be found outside Victorian pornography:

> She used to place her pretty arms about my neck, draw me to her, and laying her cheek to mine, murmur with her lips near my ear, 'Dearest, your little heart is wounded; think me not cruel because I obey the irresistible law of my strength and weakness; if your dear heart is wounded, my wild heart bleeds with yours. In the rapture of my enormous humiliation I live in your warm life, and you shall die – die, sweetly die – into mine. I cannot help it; as I draw near to you, you, in your turn, will draw near to others, and learn the rapture of that cruelty, which yet is love; so, for a

while, seek to know no more of me and mine, but trust me with all your loving spirit.'

And when she had spoken such a rhapsody, she would press me more closely in her trembling embrace, and her lips in soft kisses gently glow upon my cheek.

Laura withers and an old family friend diagnoses vampirism and identifies Carmilla as the culprit. A series of clues reveals her to be 'Mircalla', Countess Karnstein, dead (or rather undead) for a century and a half. 'Depart from this accursed ground, my poor child, as quickly as you can,' Laura is advised. 'Drive to the clergyman's house.' The necessary exhumation and exorcism by a stake through the heart is performed by the Baron Vordenburg at the Karnstein tomb:

The grave of the Countess Mircalla was opened; and the General and my father recognised each his perfidious and beautiful guest, in the face now disclosed to view. The features, though a hundred and fifty years had passed since her funeral, were tinted with the warmth of life. Her eyes were open; no cadaverous smell exhaled from the coffin.

The two medical men, one officially present, the other on the part of the promoter of the inquiry, attested the marvellous fact that there was a faint but appreciable respiration, and a corresponding action of the heart. The limbs were perfectly flexible, the flesh elastic; and the leaden coffin floated with blood, in which to a depth of seven inches, the body lay immersed.

I would advise the serious reader of *Dracula* (as would Stoker, I suspect) to whet their appetite with Le Fanu's shorter masterpiece. It adds relish. And of the multitudinous other writers of vampiric fantasia? Take your pick.

Why does the bloofer lady target children?

꠸

The 'bloofer lady' episode is introduced thus:

'The Westminster Gazette', 25 September.
A HAMPSTEAD MYSTERY.

The neighbourhood of Hampstead is just at present exercised with a series of events which seem to run on lines parallel to those of what was known to the writers of headlines as 'The Kensington Horror', or 'The Stabbing Woman', or 'The Woman in Black'. During the past two or three days several cases have occurred of young children straying from home or neglecting to return from their playing on the Heath. In all these cases the children were too young to give any properly intelligible account of themselves, but the consensus of their excuses is that they had been with a 'bloofer lady'. It has always been late in the evening when they have been missed, and on two occasions the children have not been found until early in the following morning. It is generally supposed in the neighbourhood that, as the first child missed gave as his reason for being away that a 'bloofer lady' had asked him to come for a walk, the others had picked up the phrase and used it as occasion served. This is the more natural as the favourite game of the little ones at present is luring each other away by wiles. A correspondent writes us that to see some of the tiny tots pretending to be the 'bloofer lady' is supremely funny. Some of our caricaturists might, he says, take a lesson in the irony of grotesque by comparing the reality and the picture. It is only in accordance with general principles of human nature that the 'bloofer lady' should be the popular role at these *al fresco* performances. Our correspondent naively says that even Ellen Terry could not be so winningly attractive as some of these grubby-faced little children pretend – and even imagine themselves – to be.

Superficially the passage has a number of points of interest for Dracula nit-pickers. The *Westminster Gazette* was launched in January 1893, with considerable fanfare and complaint about its sensationalism. Stoker spoofs it smartly. The proprietor was George Newnes. He is remembered principally as the founder of *Tit Bits*, a weekly which broke 'entertaining' stories of the day into fragments for mass consumption.* This is one of the few substantive date markers we have for the 1893 action of *Dracula*. A very interesting nit.

....

* The *Westminster* took a more sober turn under J.A. Spender a few years later, becoming a major political force in Britain.

Another interesting detail is Bram Stoker's revealing his theatrical self, as manager of the Lyceum, via the reference to the company's renowned star actress, Ellen Terry. She was also Henry Irving's mistress, and in the 1880s gossip about the couple's immorality had obstructed Irving's getting a knighthood (it eventually came his way in 1895).

What, though, about Lucy's vampiric interest in the very young? One can start by looking at one of the more awkward scenes in the novel, Mina embracing the bereaved Arthur, the affianced of her best friend, in what would, to the uninformed eye, look like a romantic embrace.

Victorian gentleman did not routinely dive into ladies' bosoms. But Arthur's tears, as Mina explains, wash away conventional decorum. Her breast is his:

In an instant the poor dear fellow was overwhelmed with grief. It seemed to me that all that he had of late been suffering in silence found a vent at once. He grew quite hysterical, and raising his open hands, beat his palms together in a perfect agony of grief. He stood up and then sat down again, and the tears rained down his cheeks. I felt an infinite pity for him, and opened my arms unthinkingly. With a sob he laid his head on my shoulder and cried like a wearied child, whilst he shook with emotion.

We women have something of the mother in us that makes us rise above smaller matters when the mother-spirit is invoked; I felt this big sorrowing man's head resting on me, as though it were that of the baby that some day may lie on my bosom, and I stroked his hair as though he were my own child. I never thought at the time how strange it all was.

'Baby'? 'As if he were my own child'? 'Mother-spirit'? One recalls the weird sisters, guzzling the half-smothered baby in a sack Dracula has good-naturedly thrown them by way of supper. Not much mother spirit in Castle Dracula's vaults that night.

'Shoulder', one notes, becomes 'bosom' in the course of Mina's description of her succouring Arthur. What next, by way of consolation? How far would this 'new woman' go? *Dracula* is one of those novels in which one is always pressing hard on the imagination's brake pedal.

Meanwhile, as Mina gives Arthur her breast, the not yet quite dead Lucy has converted her mother spirit into sucking the blood out of a gang of Hampstead children. It is a kind of reverse nursing – not giving suck but taking it. One wonders, of course, why these urchins are roaming Hampstead Heath by night for any vampire to have a go at them. It is odd. Then, as now, the heath's unfenced, unlit, largely unpathed wilderness was, by night, a place where daylight morals of London were relaxed.

Dracula, we must conclude, is a novel in which the fairer sex's 'mother spirit' morphs in strange ways. What is in vampire-Lucy's mind in the Hampstead scene? We know from her deathbed scene that she aspires to kiss Arthur and render him her mate; thereafter, they can enjoy family life with their 'children' on the heath. Forever.

Why did Henry Irving not bite?

꩜

Discussion of Henry Irving's influence on Bram Stoker, and on the character of the Count (see page 12 and elsewhere), raises thoughts about the great actor's involvement with *Dracula*. More precisely, his brutally curt refusal to get at all involved and help his long-serving manager, then in serious financial difficulty.*

Irving was Stoker's god. Bram dedicated his life to him – for £22 a week. Irving gave nothing emotional in return to his manager and, as a terminal slap, left him nothing in his will when he died in 1905. Irving could have helped the author of *Dracula* and did not. Stoker devoted much of his later life to a two-volume hagiography of Irving. Irving's refusal to help with *Dracula* does not appear in it, nor the slightest criticism.

At some difficulty Stoker had rushed on to paper a read-through acting version of his novel. It was performed at the Lyceum, by the theatre's actors, a week before the novel's publication, on 26 May 1897. This constituted 'performance',

....

* The dedication of the novel is to 'my dear friend Hommy-Beg' – a nickname of the novelist and dramatist Hall Caine, who loaned the distressed Stoker a much-needed £1,000.

even though it was to an audience of two people. Performance duly ensured copyright protection. Since 1894, it was international copyright protection.

Irving declined to take part in the performance, or to consider a Lyceum production. He is plausibly supposed to have explained with one word, after a brief glance at the text: 'Dreadful'.* Reportedly said to his face, it must have been one of the lower moments in Stoker's life. A stake through the heart, one might say.

Dreadful or not, the sham performance was the sensible thing to do in order to prevent stage (and imminently film) piracy. That protection would prove useful, in later years, to the widowed Florence.

Had he taken the lead part and put the play on Irving could have done wonderful things. Among his specialisms were sinister villainy (his Mephisto, famously) and great stage effects. As Hilary Spurling muses:

> [Irving] thought nothing of constructing an entire Gothic cathedral on stage at the Lyceum Theatre, installing a bluebell wood or hiring the Brigade of Guards to fight his mock battles. For Goethe's *Faust*, he had 400 ropes backstage, each with its own name and function, to raise devils, spirits and apparitions. He obliterated his actors under sumptuous costumes,

---

* See https://www.bl.uk/romantics-and-victorians/articles/bram-stokers-stage-adaptation-of-dracula#sthash.JEr4SDGW.dpuf

obstructed them with cumbersome scenery and blinded them with bolts of lightning.*

What Stoker had done with *Dracula* was tailor-made for Irving. Irving wanted no part of it.

It was an egotistic and, in the event, foolish act on the great man's part. There were factors. His reputation and health were failing. His operatic style of acting was out of style. The witty chatter of Wilde and Shaw was what audiences wanted. He was 59 years old and had nearly crippled himself in December 1896, slipping down some steps. He was perhaps fearful that Dracula might be too physical for him. Climbing like a 'lizard' up and down castle walls could not have appealed.

Stoker's own situation, following disastrous investments, was similarly parlous in 1897. Both men would have received a late-career boost from a full-blooded performance of *Dracula*. As it was, when their theatre burned down in 1898 their professional lives went with it. Irving had a stroke and died shortly afterwards; Stoker faded, under the debilitating influence of tertiary syphilis, it is suggested, writing ever worse fiction.

Why would Irving not even give a second look at *Dracula?* Irving's biographers portray a man of narcissism and *froideur* – something inseparable from his self-control on stage. He would yield no credit, proffer no generosity (even verbally) to those who served him – even a man who had served him so devotedly

....

* https://www.theguardian.com/books/2008/sep/07/history.theatre.books

as Bram Stoker. No wonder Irving's performance of *Richard III* was so admired. Like Shakespeare's villain king, Henry Irving was never in the 'giving vein'.

What, then was Bram Stoker? Irving's Renfield, it has been suggested. And, like Renfield, broken by his master. But loyal to the end.

Nosferatu?
What does that mean?

～✣～

The word 'nosferatu' is mentioned twice in *Dracula*. The first time is by Van Helsing talking, garrulously as ever, to Holmwood:

> Friend Arthur, if you had met that kiss which you know of before poor Lucy die; or again, last night when you open your arms to her, you would in time, when you had died, have become *nosferatu*, as they call it in Eastern Europe, and would all time make more of those Un-Deads that so have fill us with horror.

The second time the word 'nosferatu' crops up is again by the gabby Dutch professor:

> The *nosferatu* do not die like the bee when he sting once. He is only stronger; and being stronger, have yet more power to work evil.

Stoker himself did no research himself on the N-word. He picked it up from Emily Gerard, who waxes eloquently on it, in her articles and books – motherlode for Stoker:

More decidedly evil, however, is the vampire, or nosferatu, in whom every Roumenian peasant believes as firmly as he does in heaven or hell.

There are two sorts of vampires – living and dead. The living vampire is in general the illegitimate offspring of two illegitimate persons, but even a flawless pedigree will not ensure anyone against the intrusion of a vampire into his family vault, since every person killed by a nosferatu becomes likewise a vampire after death, and will continue to suck the blood of other innocent people till the spirit has been exorcised, either by opening the grave of the person suspected and driving a stake through the corpse, or firing a pistol shot into the coffin. In very obstinate cases it is further recommended to cut off the head and replace it in the coffin with the mouth filled with garlic, or to extract the heart and burn it, strewing the ashes over the grave. That such remedies are often resorted to, even in our enlightened days, is a well-attested fact, and there are probably few Roumenian villages where such has not taken place within the memory of the inhabitants.

This was rich pickings for Bram Stoker. But as regards the word 'nosferatu' Gerard (and, following faithfully in her wake, Stoker) got it entirely wrong. Bluntly, the word does not exist in Romanian or any other language known to etymology. Whatever 'every' Transylvanian peasant, in their ineffable ignorance believes, 'nosferatu' is not the word they apply to it.*

The once non-existent word is now world famous. Thereby hangs a tale and some instructive cultural history. Despite its publisher's advertising claim that there were nine editions in its first ten years *Dracula* was not, for its first decade, a run-away international bestseller. It would, of course, have helped its take-off if Henry Irving had done something for the stage adaptation Stoker humbly offered him.

Florence Stoker, who would survive Bram by a quarter of a century, was dogged in the financially hard-pressed years of her widowhood in the safeguarding of the copyright of *Dracula*. She forbade all stage and film adaptation, aided by the copyright protection Bram had ensured by his prophylactic, pre-publication performance in May 1897.

It was a mistake. Performance, particularly to the silent film world's audiences, would have raised *Dracula* if not from the grave then from its second-division obscurity in the Edwardian period.

What injected new life into *Dracula* was a literary crime. Intellectual property theft, the lawyers call it. The theft was perpetrated by a German film director, Albin Grau, who decided to film the novel. He had a personal reason. Serving in the First World War, with blood everywhere, he met a Serbian who claimed to be the son of a vampire. It stuck in Grau's mind. One does not meet such a person every day.

....

* The editors of Dracula's notes suggest it is a garbled version of *nosophoros*, Greek for 'plague carrier', or the Romanian *necuratul*, meaning 'devil'.

After the war Grau co-founded a German movie company called Prana-Film. The firm's launch venture was *Dracula*, under a different name. Grau may honestly have felt free to help himself. The novel's publication was two decades in the past; there had been no German-language edition until 1908. Or perhaps he carelessly neglected to enquire about getting the rights from the estate's holder, Florence Stoker. He was too busy making the film. Either way, he clearly had some apprehension. To throw any legal hounds off his tracks he renamed the story *Nosferatu: A Symphony of Horror* ('*Nosferatu: Eine Symphonie des Grauens*').

After months of hype, the picture had its lavish premiere at the Marble Hall of the Berlin Zoological Gardens on 4 March 1922. So lavish was the event that it is reckoned to have virtually ruined Prana-Film financially.

The film was directed by a master of the silent film craft, F.W. Murnau, in German expressionist style. The film is imbued with the fluent pessimisms (and arrant secularism) of Schopenhauer, whom Murnau admired extravagantly. The narrative is relocated to early 19th-century Lubeck. Castle scenes were shot in Slovakia.

Count Dracula becomes Graf Orlok. He is cat-clawed, long-toothed, bat-eared and extravagantly slovenly in dress. Tuxes are many planets away.

Lucy and Van Helsing are removed (exit, dear old wind-shovel) without perceptible narrative loss. A number of hanging threads in the novel are tidied up for the tight economy of a 90-minute film. But there is no question that what we are watching on screen is anything but a faithful adaptation of Stoker's story. It's difference is that it is not 'Englished', as Hamilton Deane's authorised version was, two years later.*

Murnau's vampire was played by the wonderfully named Max Schreck (German for 'Max Terror'). The film is in the public domain nowadays and easily available on YouTube. A useful adjunct is *Shadow of the Vampire* (2000), whose plot investigates the complex relationship of Murnau (played by John Malkovich) and Schreck (played by Willem Dafoe).

Nosferatu is an acknowledged masterpiece of silent film and a high point of Murnau's achievement. Many of its scenic effects – the shadow on the stairs, for example – are iconic. Other stills are as eye-catching, and blood-curdling, as Munch's 'The Scream'.†

It was *Nosferatu* which pioneered – in contradiction to Stoker's text, and traditional lore – the myth that vampires are mortally vulnerable to sunlight. In film versions the destruction by sunlight makes for a horrific climax. The 1958 Hammer film version could not get past the BBFC censor of the time, and had to be trimmed. I remember nonetheless shivering to the sight of Christopher Lee melting in Colchester's Playhouse. I'm not sure I did not have to lie about my age to get into the cinema. I recall sitting through two showings, afternoon and evening.

....

* I am indebted here and later in this entry to Mark Mancini, http://mentalfloss.com/article/84080/11-nightmarish-facts-about-nosferatu
† Munch did a striking picture of 'The Vampire' in 1902. The predator is female.

There was another bootleg film version of Stoker's novel in 1922 called *Dracula's Death*. No record of it remains, other than one 'still'. It does not suggest posterity has suffered any great loss.

Nosferatu was lucky not to suffer the same oblivion as *Dracula's Death*, which would indeed have been a great loss. A month after the lavish Berlin launch, someone anonymously sent Florence Stoker a programme in which the self-incriminating words 'freely adapted from Bram Stoker's *Dracula*' were printed.

The 62-year-old Florence had not been aware of the film's conception, production or release. She mustered all the institutional forces at her disposal to protect the property which provided her living. She sued in Germany on clear grounds of copyright infringement (the novel was protected by international copyright law for 28 years, except in the US). The case dragged on for three years, over which period Florence sanctioned the Hamilton Deane production of *Dracula* for the London stage. It was hugely successful.

Prana-Film was bankrupted having embarked on a string of bad business decisions – not the least of which were the marketing campaign for its first film, and its legal defence. Not a single mark of damages was in prospect for the injured Stoker estate. Undeterred, Florence went on to demand all copies of the film be destroyed. A German court, in 1925, duly ordered every surviving copy be burned. It was an extraordinary sentence. One can see it as a harbinger of how the National Socialist authorities, under Goebbels, would deal with films which offended the Party.

A single copy in France, legend has it, escaped the flames and made its way to the US in 1929 where *Dracula* was not protected by copyright law. As Mark Mancini records:

> Thus, the undead picture haunted Florence Stoker until the end of her days. Before she died in 1937, a handful of screenings took place – usually in the United States. Stoker relentlessly tracked down wayward copies of the movie and incinerated those that she got her hands on. But despite her best efforts, *Nosferatu* lived on in the form of pirated bootlegs.

In 1984 a pristine uncut copy was discovered. It was relaunched, coloured, in Berlin, with great pomp and ceremony. It can currently be found on YouTube.

Why does Dracula take risks?
(Dr Freud explains)

༄༅

It makes for an interesting novel, of course, but the motivation is curious. Why, when he arrives 'discreetly' at Whitby, evading the major ports' customs officials, does Dracula come in a vessel, all of whose crew he kills, including the captain, leaving the ship to wash up wrecked on Whitby sands, accompanied over the next few days by a stream of bloodless corpses? This is discreet? It is the biggest thing to happen in Whitby since the Vikings destroyed the Abbey.

Did Dracula not foresee arrival amid mystery and watery holocaust might raise some public notice? At the very least a headline or two in the local Northumbrian press?

When he buys up dozens of properties in London and a large estate in Purfleet, he does so under the name 'Count De Ville'. He might as well call himself 'His Satanic Majesty'.

Renfield, his 'servant', knows that his 'Master' is a few thousand yards away. Dracula knows he knows. Who, in their right mind, would entrust their safety to a certified homicidal fly-eating maniac? Renfield does, of course, eventually, betray Dracula and his location. Judas Renfield.

What a security-conscious Dracula would do is lie low, just making the occasional night excursion to keep the blood flowing. Then, in ten years, strike – like his ancestor, the Scourge of God. If he plays his cards right he will, like Attila, conquer the world.

Tourism in London is never as easy for the foreigner as the advertisements promise. Attempting it with 50 pieces of baggage, each weighing several hundredweight of Romanian dirt ('Anything to declare, sir?') would, one would think, necessitate extreme caution. The fact is, Dracula is hugely vulnerable. As Van Helsing points out, all you have to do is put a wild rose on his coffin while he enjoys his daytime snooze, and he's coffined for eternity. And a very nasty eternity it will be. Or, if roses are out of season, a blast from Quincey's Winchester into the coffin will do the trick (if decapitation and the wooden stake seem too messy).

Dracula can't enter houses unless invited. It will be difficult to have any kind of social life in Britain with that restriction. Is the no-entry-unless-invited bar the same with railway compartments, public lavatories, the British Museum reading room? Dracula is simply not wired for London. He is asocial.

Why, then, does Dracula imperil himself? He's got a lot to lose by coming to England. Eternal life is top of the list of things he can lose. But risk himself he does. It is clearly a motivated and long-planned thing, not mere recklessness. But it is hard to put one's finger on what his underlying motive and plan are. Van Helsing would, in his irritatingly know-all way, explain that Dracula is what he calls a 'man-child'. He hasn't grown up and realised the dangers every adult is wary of. He is cunning but stupid. An odd mixture.

Dr Freud was practising in Vienna at the time of *Dracula*. He solved the rat-man enigma. Could he do the same for the bat-man? Let us imagine the sage's analysis of the Count on his couch (I have foreborne writing it in the German the two of them would speak, apart from key terminology):

The subject Dracula manifests, floridly, all the symptoms of the narcissist (*Narzissmus*) – despite the fact that he will never see his own imago (*selbstild*). Mirrors, reflective surfaces (such as water, burnished metal), paint and canvas, the most modern camera *technik*, all throw back nothing. Leonardo could not picture him. He himself does not know what he looks like. This creates an acute identity crisis (*Identitätskrise*). That crisis forces him, irresistibly, to protestive assertiveness (*Protestive Durchsetzbarkeit*) even at the risk of self-destruction. Man sans imago is torment Lucifer himself might have reserved for the damned most deserving of psychic pain. Count Dracula will be in that pain for as long as he lives.

What could be clearer?

What do Stoker's notes tell us?

༈

Who knows where and when *Dracula* was conceived?
Possibly, some have speculated, after reading *Carmilla*,
when Le Fanu's novel came out in 1872. Possibly while watching, from the wings, Henry Irving shivering the audience's
timbers with his famed performance of Mephisto. Irving seems
somewhere in the novel's DNA; many critics have noted that.
Perhaps Stoker's first reading of *Dr Jekyll and Mr Hyde* planted
another seed.

The usual (highly dubious) explanation where Gothic fiction is concerned is a dream. Sure enough, Bram's son, Noel
Stoker, said that inspiration had come to his father 'in a nightmarish dream after eating too much dressed crab'. All writers
of horror stories should dine on it.

The first layer of Stoker's surviving notes were dashed
down in early summer 1890. We know that because Stoker
dated some of his earliest memoranda. They were scrawled
in his notoriously illegible handwriting on whatever piece of
paper came to hand. There were certainly many more jottings
than have survived.

Two things are established by the following first page of
surviving memoranda: (1) that it was a novel of ideas, not a
mere 'shilling shocker'; and (2) that it could have developed

from its starting point in interestingly different ways. This is what we find on the first page:

Lawyer – Aaronson purchase
[ditto] – (Sortes Virgilianae) conveyance of body
[ditto] – purchase old house town
Lawyer's clerk – goes to Ge [sic] Styria
Mad doctor – loves girl
Mad patient – theory of perpetual life
Philosophic historian
Undertaker
Undertaker's man
Girl – dies
Lawyer's shrewd sceptical sister
Crank
German professor of history
Maid engaged undertaker's man
Silent man & dumb woman – Count's servants
London in power of Count some terrible fear – man
    knows secret
Detective inspector

It is clear from the outset Stoker foresaw major outlines – but not, at this primal stage, the vampire's name. If the novel had a title in his mind it was probably 'The Un-Dead' or 'The Dead Un-Dead'. Lawyer's business opens the novel as it does in the published text – but Jonathan Harker and his employer, Mr Hawkins of Exeter, are not, like Aaronson, Jewish. And why Dracula should have chosen these countrified solicitors is never explained to the reader. Exeter does not figure in the action. It is not even one of the places Dracula deposits his 50 boxes of earth. Stoker may have held it in reserve as a possible bolthole for his villain-hero late in the action, and then never used it.

'Sortes Virgilianae' is a fortune-telling phrase. It denotes opening the works of Virgil to receive instruction or foresee the future (there are variations including other major works, e.g. the *Iliad*, the Bible). What Stoker means by it here is elusive.

'Conveyance of the body' is, recognisably, a main element in the story. Plausibly getting Dracula's (in)human remains and his impedimenta from the Carpathian wilderness to Carfax Abbey without official frontier obstruction proves a narrative challenge.

One notes that Stoker's first intention was that Dracula should establish his HQ in an appropriately old London house. In the event it is rural Carfax, in Purfleet, Essex, with as many as 49 boxes of soil potentially distributed around inner London (is Dracula using multiple solicitors?). Carfax, a dilapidated country house with a ruined chapel attached, adjoins the thriving private lunatic asylum managed by John ('Jack') Seward. The asylum contains the Count's 'index', Renfield, who throbs violently when his Master is in the vicinity: a kind of vampiric tuning fork.

The 'philosophic historian' never made it into the novel – his part was swallowed up by the omniscient Van Helsing, a thinker of many more parts than mere philosophy. As he is only too willing to demonstrate. Continuously. The 'crank' and Harker's sister also fall by the narrative wayside. But at this early stage Stoker was clear about the centrality of girls' deaths to his novel. He wanted female readers, as well as male. He got them.

In a flash, Stoker has also seen how the novel will begin: with a jump-start – a lawyer's clerk en route to Transylvania. The crossed out 'Ge' records the intention – elaborated in later notes – for a long episode in Munich, with its 'house of the dead' (city mortuary), and complicated doings with a dead or undead body (see below, page 108, for more on this dropped sub-plot).

'Styria' indicated Stoker's indebtedness to Le Fanu's *Carmilla*, which is set there. Stoker changed the setting to make his debt less obvious. Styria was and is in Austria. It, and its capital Graz, was, in the 1890s, hooked into modern transport systems and European life. Had he stuck with Styria Stoker would have had to antedate his narrative, as did Le Fanu, to the early 19th century. Dracula, viz typewriters, telephones, voice recorders, and Kodak cameras, is very firmly set in the period in which Stoker was writing and publishing. 1893 is the putative date of Dracula's great raid on England.

It is not stated whether the 'undertaker' and his girl are in Munich or London; but deducibly it is the latter. In the novel as written Dracula has no servants – merely hired help. Servants would have been useful: particularly if deaf and dumb. But it might have been a touch too Gothic for London, 1893. One can hardly see how the post would be advertised. 'Wanted: Two Entirely Useless House Servants.'

One perceives in the last clutch of notes on this page the outline of a novel that never happened. Let us, fancifully, construct that novel from the fragments Stoker has left us.

In London the newly arrived Dracula employs the services of an undertaker to move his body. The undertaker's assistant's fiancée is victimised by the Count. The Count's servants divulge things. They are frightened. So is London. There have been a spate of killings in the capital – it is Jack the Ripper all over again. The police are called in, a crack Scotland Yard detective sets out to solve the case – hopefully brighter than Conan Doyle's Inspector Lestrade.

One should remember that the period Stoker was writing – 1890 to 1895 – was the high point of Sherlock mania. Detectives, amateur or professional, were the rage. Oddly, however, no policeman sets foot in *Dracula*. Why? Stoker, I suspect, made the honest analysis that it was not his métier. He had not the cleverness as a writer. Leave crime and detection to the much cleverer Conan Doyle. A writer should know his limitations.

The first page of notes is scrappy, but it discloses a mind fizzing with ideas, carving the novel that became *Dracula* out of raw material. The insight into the author's creative process is a privilege.

How much German does Jonathan speak?

⨳

In the first pages of the novel, the point is made that Jonathan has only a 'smattering' of the language at his command. The extent of this is vague. The uncertainty, though, fulfils a useful function, allowing as it does a variable level of comprehension/non-comprehension in the German exchanges.

The matter of Jonathan's linguistic ability – or lack thereof – was in fact in Stoker's mind going back to his earliest thinking about 'The Un-Dead', the story which later became *Dracula*.

He was, at its primeval stage, years before publication, mulling over versions of the novel with different plots (call them *Ur-Draculas*). Stoker never got round to drafting them in full. But he played with them in his head over a number of years.

Stoker's first surviving note (scrawled, one can guess, in March 1890) is: 'Aaronson purchase'. The Jewish lawyer, Abraham Aaronson, returns later in the unlovely depiction of the lawyer Emanuel Hildesheim. Stoker, via Mina's journal, describes him as 'a Hebrew of rather the Adelphi Theatre type, with a nose like a sheep, and a fez'.*

....

* Stoker recalls the *Jewish Chronicle's* protest at the 1889 production of Pettit and Sims's *London Day by Day* at the Adelphi, for its 'hideous caricature' of Jews.

Following scant jottings we can put together a narrative line which never quite made it into printed existence. Dracula is negotiating – by mail, the notes record – for 'purchase old house town' [*sic*]. Something appropriately ancient in London. It appears, from a later note, the Count chose the property himself by stabbing a copy of the law directory, selecting from it the property where the point of his dagger lands.

This unusual purchase method was dropped in the printed text. Dracula ends up buying not an ancient town house but a rural estate, with consecrated ground around its ruined church. It is located near Purfleet, Essex, and next to the private lunatic asylum in which Renfield is confined (sometimes in a straitjacket). Carfax's features are strictly laid down by Dracula. He demands the ruined property should border a river. Since vampires have great difficulty with running water this may seem strange. As Van Helsing says, 'The Count, even if he takes the form of a bat, cannot cross the running water of his own volition'. This oddity is not, I think, explained.

In this primal layer of the novel, it is the Count himself, not the junior lawyer and his mysteriously unwell senior, Mr Hawkins, who locates the site from which he will launch his great attack on London – using, presumably, other of his properties as 'safe houses' in central London as the campaign requires. The Martian vampire attack fantasised by H.G. Wells and published in the same year as *Dracula*, 1897, will be nothing in comparison to what the vampire plans.

The London lawyer (Aaronson, until he becomes the

gentile, Exeter-based, Hawkins) has a 'shrewd, skeptical sister'. She never materialises. The deal is clinched by a 'Letter to Aaronson from Count _____ [the name Dracula had not yet been hit on] Styria asking to come or send trustworthy law[yer] who does not speak German'.

It is a highly odd instruction for a client with, himself, imperfect English to make. At this stage, one notes, Stoker intended to follow Le Fanu's *Carmilla* and set his novel in Styria, German-speaking Austria, as it now is. Why, then, insist on a lawyer unable speak the native tongue? It would surely be vital to negotiating any legal conveyancing, money exchange, and the transmission of funds Harker has been sent out specifically to execute.

The first answer that comes to mind is because the Count does not want the proto-Harker capable of asking questions en route about grisly doings in and around his castle. Jonathan, despite losing a handsome commission, might think a client who lives on human blood and abducts babies in sacks a somewhat undesirable customer for the firm of Hawkins and Harker. In the published text, with the setting transposed to Transylvania, the point is made that Harker simply does not understand the dire warnings he gets at the way-stage inn from the innkeeper and his wife. But since they are now talking Romanian, his knowledge of German is neither here nor there.

Jonathan's limited German, then, can be seen as largely a hangover from the expunged Styria setting, retained because it continued to serve a purpose to the author. Stoker himself did not speak German and, given his pressing theatrical duties, he did not have time to lard his narrative with the Germanic touches and colouring his narrative would need if his hero, and the Count, were speaking that language.

Why Whitby?

~~~

Dracula and his creator have been commemorated in a number of places: in Jack Straw's Castle, the majestic pub off Hampstead Heath, for example, where the vampire hunters gather their strength before breaking open Lucy's tomb and doing worse things.

Romania has built up a thriving tourist industry. But it has had its hiccups getting there. The communist government, in the 1980s, banned Draculite tourism and any use of the word for commercial purposes. Stoker's vampire was regarded, not unreasonably, as a symbol of decadent, blood-sucking capitalism. Nothing for a proud nation to glorify.

Estimates reckon there are 70,000 Romanian workers currently (early 1917 as I write) in London. In my experience they weary very quickly of 'the Dracula conversation'. Who can blame them?

After the fall of communism the Dracula industry reasserted itself in Romania. In 2000 the Romanian government made it official, projecting a multi-million dollar Dracula Park. Blood-flavoured shakes were again on the menu. Conferences and world festivals are held in what used to be Transylvania. Hotels were positively encouraged to Draculise themselves and their services.

Far away, the other thriving resort which has made a fortune out of its Dracula associations is the northern town of Whitby, which today offers attractions such as 'The Dracula Experience', the Bram Stoker International Film Festival, and Whitby Goth Weekend.

There was a vast library about vampirism, even in the 1890s, which Stoker didn't read. He relied, centrally, on a few standby books for background. He had no first-hand acquaintance of his novel's foreign setting. Far-flung as many of the Lyceum tours were (five to the US, for example) the company never ventured into Transylvania.

But Stoker thought deeply, for many years, about the book he was writing. As has been said, first ideas began to stir in his mind, one suspects, in the mid- to late 1880s, with Henry Irving's barnstorming performance of Mephisto in *Faust*; Gerard's 1885 essay on Transylvanian folklore which, plausibly, Stoker came across; and Robert Louis Stevenson's *The Strange Case of Dr Jekyll and Mr Hyde*, which Stoker must have read when it came out in 1886, pointing to new possibilities for gothic fiction. I have sometimes thought that in the far distance of Stoker's mind he meditated a Dr Jekyll and Mr Hyde plot centred on Dr Seward and Mr Renfield. One can fantasise how it might go. I don't think any novelist has.

The breakthrough event in the creation of *Dracula* was Whitby, July–August 1890. Stoker holidayed there, with his family – Florence and son Noel – after a disappointing Lyceum tour in Scotland. Some rest and recuperation were needed.

Stoker had time that summer to explore the town. There is history in every flagstone and brick. He listened to the talk of locals, whose Yorkshire patois, unchanged since the middle ages, delighted him. Stoker had a wonderful ear. In Whitby's public library he came across what would be the novel's seminal text, William Wilkinson's *An Account of the Principalities of Wallachia and Moldavia* (1820). A hard read, one might think from the title. But on this occasion, inspirational. Wilkinson and Whitby together formulated what would be the framework and the founding idea of *Dracula*.

Walking the town, as one likes to fantasise, Stoker hit on the idea of the young heroines, former school friends, meeting up for a reunion holiday in Whitby. They are both on the brink of the great change in their lives. Mina (Murray) has left school teaching to unleash her 'man's brain' as a New Woman typewriter girl. Lucy, the avatar of traditional maidenhood, has received, aged nineteen, three eminently eligible proposals of marriage. Which shall she accept? The doctor, the Lord, or the American adventurer? Lucky Lucy.

Not lucky for long. Also in on the Whitby party is the uninvited guest from Transylvania. There are plausible reasons for Dracula choosing to make his entry to England in this port. Invaders, since the Danes in the 9th century, have arrived on Whitby's shores to do their worst. The town's ancient ruins tell the stories in crumbling stone.

The town's inhabitants recalled something relatively recent – the wreck of the Russian schooner, the *Dmitri* of Narva, in October 1885. The vessel foundered on Whitby harbour's notoriously tricky sand bar, in a terrible storm. The whole crew drowned.

Photographs were taken by Frank Meadow Sutcliffe. They were sold for years after as postcards and Stoker would have seen them. Stoker surely heard the local myth that wrongly claimed the ship had a cargo of coffins, which washed up, along with sailors' corpses, for days after the storm subsided. In fact the *Dmitri* was carrying a cargo of silver sand – near enough to Dracula's 50 boxes of sacred dirt.

The Russian ship's dramatic end, as preserved and embellished in local lore, gave Stoker valuable plot machinery. In the novel the *Dmitri* becomes the *Demeter*, from Varna. Why Whitby? Had Dracula come to one of Britain's main ports of entry – Dover or Southampton, for example – there would have been customs and immigration officials, curious to see his papers (if he assumed human form for the occasion), asking awkward questions about why a count would need 50 large boxes of Romanian dirt.

Dracula's solution is ingenious. If he arrives in a wrecked Russian vessel and leaps on shore as a large dog there will be no questions asked of him. He has done the necessary research on Whitby. A mad dog running through the streets of Dover would be shot in no time. The Contagious Diseases (Animals) Act had been introduced, as a preventive against rabies (particularly from abroad). It would have been a humiliating end for Count Dracula, lineal descendant of Attila the Hun.

Whitby imposed no such barriers. Dracula can hide (and feed), four-legged, in the local woods until the arrangements he has made for the transport of his all-important boxes are put in train via the Great Western Railway.

From photographs and letters (written in script he can understand) he knows about the delectable Mina, which makes Whitby all the more desirable. Stoker does not describe the last voyage of the *Demeter* in detail, but the reader can reconstruct Dracula's plan. It's smart.

He kills the crew, one by one. They do not examine what is in the boxes; they are too frightened. Their bodies are thrown overboard. Dracula can create a microclimate – the Devil taught him how to do this in the Scholasticon (see 'How Dead Is Dracula?', page 9) – and the ship is forced to battle through neverending fog and storm.

The captain, the last surviving human on board, true to his command, lashes himself to the wheel and leaves a log-book record of what has happened – insofar as he has understood it. Dracula lets him survive until the boat is wrecked. Why? Because were he gone, by the laws of salvage the boat and its cargo would belong to whoever next boarded it. That would not be good for the all-important boxes. Horrible thought: they might just be emptied out and dumped on Whitby Sands.

It all fit. One can almost see where Stoker assembled some of the key components. A bench on the cliff path, atop the 199 steps to St Mary's Church, which the mad dog Dracula bounds up, is inscribed with the words: 'The view from this spot inspired Bram Stoker'. Quite likely so.

Stoker put down quantities of notes about Whitby, its dialect, and the *Dmitri* wreck. His sense of narrative was always tactically fluid. He must, I suspect, have toyed with the idea of setting the whole of his novel, or at least all the English chapters, in Whitby.

But like Irving, he always went big. 'Dracula destroys Whitby' would have been small. But the coastal town supplies a useful springboard; even if, for some readers, there is too much of gabby Mr Swales.

What is the point of
R.M. Renfield?

ᵒᵍᵏᵕ

It is a question pondered by many readers, all adaptors of *Dracula*, and vegans. The majority of us are meat eaters, consumers of things that were once, like us, alive and kicking. But few would follow the 'zoophagous' Renfield's diet. The 'fly-eater' (as Stoker bluntly called the madman in his notes) graduates to death's head moths, to spiders, to sparrows (munched raw, with feathers). In prospect are bird-eating kittens if the asylum is willing to serve them up. Alive. How long, wonders Dr Seward, before his patient graduates to live human meat? The very idea – and the temptation to give Renfield his head – draws Seward into strange waters:

> What would have been [Renfield's] later steps? It would almost be worth while to complete the experiment. It might be done if there were only a sufficient cause. Men sneered at vivisection, and yet look at its results to-day! Why not advance science in its most difficult and vital aspect – the knowledge of the brain? Had I even the secret of one such mind – did I hold the key to the fancy of even one lunatic – I might advance

my own branch of science to a pitch compared with which Burdon-Sanderson's physiology or Ferrier's brain-knowledge would be as nothing. If only there were a sufficient cause! I must not think too much of this, or I may be tempted; a good cause might turn the scale with me, for may not I too be of an exceptional brain, congenitally?*

Renfield, for Seward, is an object of clinical study as much as a patient requiring care. He is man experimentally eating his way upward through various species, creating his own evolutionary narrative. One can see, in embryo, a different novel from that which Stoker eventually published.

This is all very interesting. But it does not answer the question of why Stoker gave so much space to the zoophagite character in a novel about vampirism. And nowhere in that space is it explained how Renfield and Dracula become personally acquainted – if, indeed, in the flesh they ever do, until Dracula drops by the asylum to kill his slave.

That Renfield was in Stoker's mind from his first conception of the novel, in summer 1890, is demonstrable. His first page of 1890 notes has, as its fifth and six items:

Mad Doctor – loves girl
Mad patient – theory of perpetual life

---

* John Burdon-Sanderson and David Ferrier were actual living scientists.

The editors of Stoker's notes speculate that at the primal stage, Jack Seward and Renfield may have been conceived as the same character. If so, the idea was dropped in subsequent composition. Renfield's big endeavour is 'perpetual life', which he somehow knows the vampire has achieved. Renfield wants it and will destroy life to get it. At present that means insect and arachnid life and one luckless bird.

What, substantially, do we know about Renfield's background? He is orphanic – although someone must be paying the bills at Seward's private asylum. We know his initials, 'R.M.', but not his Christian names (if, at this stage of life, he is still Christian). The name Renfield itself in Stoker's notes was a late addition to the narrative, alternating with 'Renfold'. In *Carmilla* (see page 43), 'Bertha Rheinfeldt' is one of Carmilla's historic victims. But, the echo of the names apart, the connection tells us only what we already knew. Stoker knew, liked and was indebted to Le Fanu's novel.

Renfield's CV is murky. This is how Dr Seward profiles him in his medical notes:

R. M. Renfield, aetat 59. Sanguine temperament, great physical strength, morbidly excitable, periods of gloom, ending in some fixed idea which I cannot make out. I presume that the sanguine temperament itself and the disturbing influence end in a mentally-accomplished finish, a possibly dangerous man, probably dangerous if unselfish.

Renfield, it surprises one to know, is elderly: he is routinely played younger on screen. That he is 'sanguine' has passing interest. It means, in terms of the humoristic theory of medicine (long outdated in 1890) that 'blood' predominates in his character. The sanguine person is social, talkative, exuberant. When blood is spilled on the floor, from Seward's arm which Renfield has cut in a maniac moment, he laps it up. Thereafter he seems to know everything Seward knows. He owns him.

Renfield is clever, well bred and well educated. That point is made, as a *coup de théâtre*, late in the narrative, when Renfield ceases being a raving lunatic and metamorphoses into a highly rational being. And in his last appearances in the narrative he is not merely 'rational' he is positively intellectual, capable of high-table graces and good conversation.

Seward, who has not previously witnessed this side of Renfield, is amazed when his patient first meets Mina, with an explosion of courtesy, erudition and compliment:

'You will, of course, understand, Mrs Harker, that when a man is so loved and honoured as our host is, everything regarding him is of interest in our little community. Dr Seward is loved not only by his household and his friends, but even by his patients, who, being some of them hardly in mental equilibrium, are apt to distort causes and effects. Since I myself have been an inmate of a lunatic asylum, I cannot but notice that the sophistic tendencies of some of its inmates lean towards the errors of *non causa* and *ignoratio elenchi.'** I [Dr Seward] positively opened my eyes at this new development. Here was my own pet lunatic – the most pronounced of his type that I had ever met with – talking elemental philosophy, and with the manner of a polished gentleman.

He is a very well-read gentleman. His elemental philosophy, so called, has a strong tincture of Ernst Haeckel, whose motto was 'ontogeny recapitulates phylogeny' (one passes, in life, through the stages of human evolution). Renfield's harping on the master/slave image, with reference to his relationship with Dracula, indicates at least a passing knowledge of Hegel's best-known image. We may presume education at a good university and, plausibly, a period of study in Germany. And a life-changing vacation in Transylvania?

In his pre-asylum days Renfield was not merely known to Arthur's father, Lord Godalming, but intimate with the nobleman. As he airily discloses, on meeting Mina and Arthur, in his cell:

> 'Lord Godalming, I had the honour of seconding your father at the Windham; I grieve to know, by your holding the title, that he is no more. He was a man loved and honoured by all who knew him; and in his youth was, I have heard, the inventor of a burnt rum punch, much patronised on Derby night.'

....
* *Non causa* and *ignoratio elenchi*: ignorance of cause and fallacious argument. Renfield has been reading Schopenhauer.

The Windham was a London club, founded in the early 19th century. The first rule for members was to be aware that the club existed 'to secure a convenient and agreeable place of meeting for a society of gentlemen, all connected with each other by a common bond of literary or personal acquaintance'. Renfield supposedly had the 'honour' of jointly proposing this knight of the realm for membership. (As is noted elsewhere – see pages 123–4 – Henry Irving was one of the Windham's most distinguished members. So, too, club correspondence confirms, was Bram Stoker, who acted as secretary.)

The Derby Day allusion – a racing meet famed for Derby Night high jinks – hints that Renfield, in his day, may have been one of the wilder men about town, fuelled by a generous intake of burnt rum punch, whatever that may be. In more serious mood he is well up with politics: capable of discussing the recent Monroe doctrine with Quincey, soon to be tested in the Spanish American war.

The most pressing puzzle is whether Renfield has made Dracula's acquaintance before the Count comes to England to take up residence in the ominous ruin Carfax, which 'abuts' the asylum. Is that abutment a coincidence? If so, it's remarkably coincidental. Did Dracula plan this contingency? A 'slave' might be very useful to him – 'a stranger in a strange land', as he calls himself (there is always an interesting touch of poetry in Dracula's speech). But, given the choice, one would not choose a slave in a straitjacket locked up in an asylum.

Renfield claims that the flies he eats are sent by Dracula. Are they somehow bearers of messages? Whatever, Renfield knows, instinctually, when Dracula arrives in England on 19 August. Harker overhears him say, as he sniffs round his cell:

> 'I am here to do Your bidding, Master. I am Your slave, and You will reward me, for I shall be faithful. I have worshipped You long and afar off. Now that You are near, I await Your commands, and You will not pass me by, will You, dear Master, in Your distribution of good things?'*

Does Dracula, when he is Renfield's next-door neighbour, meet up regularly with his 'slave' by mist, bat or rat? Their relationship is mysterious beyond the one fact that a relationship of some significant kind has been forged.

Renfield values his neighbourhood closeness to Carfax. Most of all he relishes it when his Master is in coffined residence next door. He attacks the carters taking away the Count's body in its massive box with homicidal fury. He does not, apparently, register that a new location is necessary for his master's safety. Renfield, Seward notes, is violent by day, when Dracula is in the vicinity, quiet by night. Renfield is, as Van Helsing later puts it, the 'index' of where the Count is, a radar role taken on after his death by Mina.

Dracula kills Renfield because his slave has fallen in love (as everyone seems to, on the spot) with Mina. He betrays his

....
* Note the capitalisation: Dracula is Renfield's God. Literally.

master to protect her throat from the deadly kiss. He himself is killed by assault on his own neck, not by the fang he craves but a blow, shattering his spine. He will never achieve 'perpetual life'. But then, at the end of the day, neither does Dracula. Or anyone, come to that. A solemn thought.

There are little black holes puncturing every inch of the Renfield story but, read carefully, they work to create a counterpoint; a not quite narrated story on the edge of the narrative we are reading. Renfield puzzles, but he can be defended as a thought-provoking part of the design.

Why are the Gypsies
so loyal to Dracula?

The Count is superhumanly strong. He throws Harker's luggage about as if it were eggshells. But how, to take one salient example, does he get 50 heavy boxes of good Transylvanian dirt to England, without help? It will be many days of back-breaking work, involving lurching transport, by horse and cart, over unmade roads, then complicated loading on board the cargo ship in Varna.

The point is made in the text that Dracula has no servants, domestic or manual, inside or outside of his castle. Which is why his home is in such a disgraceful state of unrepair inside and outside. We see him making the beds himself – and as I've suggested elsewhere (see page 37) he can be imagined washing his own underwear – but who does the heavy lifting around Castle Dracula?

Gypsies, in a word. Tzigany. One of the undeveloped areas of the novel is the loyalty that Dracula inspires in these unruly people, as alien in modern Transylvania as he is. Of course they 'belong' and are popularly thought to originate in Romania: what is their language? Romany. What are they called? 'Roma'. (On the other hand, 'Gypsy' hints at distantly

Egyptian beginnings. In reality, anthropological consensus puts their origin in India.) But they travel across frontiers – and are suspected of being incorrigibly criminal ('didicoys') wherever they set up their temporary living quarters. They are in the world but not of it. Like Dracula.

At various points in the narrative Gypsies are described doing this and that for their master. A desperate Harker gives one of them a letter to send back to England. A mistake. Despite Harker's monetary bribe the Gypsy gives the letter straight away to Dracula.

Why do these notoriously independent people give Dracula their allegiance? In his notes (drawing, I suspect, on Sabine Baring Gould)* Stoker jotted down a line about the Gypsy tradition of service to ruthless masters which can be traced back to Pharaoh. It would not trouble them that he was spilling blood. Or drinking it.

There were, at the time Stoker was writing and researching, some 150,000 Gypsies in Hungary, and therefore, we might reasonably think, hundreds of thousands moving nomadically across the Balkans. 'Gypsies hang on to Magyar castles,' he noted, 'and call themselves by names of the owner and profess his faith, whatever it be.' They are, as the last scene depicts, prepared to fight to the death for him.

In an informative article, Beverley Richardson notes that

---

* For Stoker's indebtedness to Baring Gould see the entry below on Dracula's hairy palms (page 142).

The ancient home of the Gypsies, India, has many mythical vampire figures. The Bhuta is the soul of a man who died an untimely death. It wandered around animating dead bodies at night and attacked the living like a ghoul. In northern India could be found the brahmaparusha, a vampire-like creature with a head encircled by intestines and a skull from which it drank blood.

The most famous Indian vampire is Kali, who had fangs,

> wore a garland of corpses or skulls and had four arms. Her temples were near the cremation grounds. She and the goddess Durga battled the demon Raktabija who could reproduce himself from each drop of blood spilled. Kali drank all his blood so none was spilled, thereby winning the battle and killing Raktabija.

There was, it is interesting to note,

> One Gypsy vampire [who] was called a mullo (one who is dead). This vampire was believed to return and do malicious things and/or suck the blood of a person (usually a relative who had caused their death, or not properly observed the burial ceremonies, or who kept the deceased's possessions instead of destroying them as was proper.)*

* http://www.thingsthatgoboo.com/monsters/vamphistorygypsies.htm

More than one needs to know perhaps. But fascinating. One can boil it down to the folkloric fact that Gypsies and vampires have a traditional affinity. And one can wonder whether, given a long enough stay in London, Dracula might recruit a new set of helpers from England's roads and encampments.

What else was happening in 1893?

꼭끞

Stoker, as his notes testify, began writing down ideas for *Dracula* in spring and summer 1890. He may have been thinking about the novel for some time before then. At any rate, it was anything but a rush job. The nineties were busy years for him, Henry Irving, and the Lyceum theatre. Finally the work was published on 26 May 1897. That year the Lyceum suffered a disastrous fire, and it had been clear for some time that Irving's stardom was fading. He was not an actor who suited *fin de siècle*.

There may also have been things happening in the book world delaying the publication of Stoker's novel. The venerable three-decker, the form of fiction which had, via the 'leviathan' circulating libraries, dominated since Walter Scott's day, was overthrown, by authors' and publishers' boycott and protest, in 1893–4. Thereafter the sleeker one-volume hardback (at a standard 6/-) took over. *Dracula* awkwardly straddled this great change historically. One only has to weigh it in one's hand to realise that it is a three-volume novel in one-volume format. Like a fat man in a too-tight waistcoat. This may have been one of the reasons it was not, on publication, a runaway bestseller. *Dracula*'s bestsellerdom had to await the knock-on effects of film and stage versions 30 years later.

While on the subject of dates, critics have argued about that of the action. A case can be made for it being a novel of the moment: 1897. But the most plausible date for the Count's failed invasion of England is a few months in spring, summer and autumn 1893. Daily and monthly dates are prominent in that Stoker has been shown to have used a calendar for that year.* Seasonally it was originally to be set in a bitter winter. Stoker changed that, one might hazard, to centre the early action on St George's Eve (4 May).

The reason for antedating the narrative four years in the past may be guessed at. 1897 was the year of the Diamond Jubilee of Queen Victoria. It would have been too distracting to have Dracula wandering into London in Jubilee turmoil: although his making an assault on the royal throat(s) is a piquant fantasy. John Brown rushes in, his *scien dhu* flashing, to save his 'little lady' from a fate worse than state funeral. It could work.

If it is 1893 (I agree it is)[†] there is barely a reference to public events in England or the US. Renfield does bring up the Monroe doctrine when he meets Quincey but does not, as he could have done, touch on the current US annexation of Hawaii as an act of imperialism.

In Stoker's notes Gladstone is mentioned. He may have thought of drawing some analogy with the 1893 prime minister, the GOM ('Grand Old Man') of British political life. Dracula,

....

* See the chronological summary on pages 99–107 for the novel's internal chronology.

[†] See also 'Why Does the Bloofer Lady Target Children?', page 46.

his country's oldest (un)living tyrant, might have been portrayed as the GOMpire of Romania. In the event Stoker decided to blank out all current political and world events. *Dracula* is a novel narrated against a featureless white background as regards history.

Nonetheless *Dracula*'s time-setting is structurally identified, very precisely, by something else. American technology. One of Stoker's early ideas, his notes tell us, was to make Quincey an American inventor. It would have fit – although for action scenes in the late narrative the Winchester-toting Texan, Stoker decided, would fit even better.

The plot of *Dracula* runs electrically on American technology, and the appliances of the greatest inventor of them all, Thomas Edison. There is, in the techno-framework, some blurring of exact years, over 1893–7. It does not jar since invention takes time to reach the market place.

Jack Seward keeps his diary not in the shorthand Jonathan uses, but on a phonic voice recorder. These machines were invented, patented and mass-marketed in the 1890s by Edison, and Seward must have been an early British adopter.

It is relevant here to quote expert description which is well beyond my personal expertise, but which I find fascinating (there is, incidentally, no lengths to which lovers of Dracula will not go in fleshing out the novel's contingencies, such as these. Good for them):

> Edison indicated that the phonograph could be used for taking dictation, recording legal testimony,

teaching languages and recording correspondence and even military orders. It seems likely that Stoker first encountered phonographic recordings while visiting Tennyson with Henry Irving in 1890, and later incorporated the technology into his novel. There are two phonographs in *Dracula*: the first belongs to Dr. Seward and is used for making clinical records; the second belongs to Lucy Westenra, presumably used for social and entertainment purposes, which Dr. Seward also employs. Jennifer Wicke suggests that Dr. Seward's phonographic diary is 'a technologized zone of the novel, inserted at a historical point where phonography was not widespread'; however, Edison had invented the original tin foil phonograph in 1877 and the more recent wax cylinder model described by Stoker in *Dracula* was invented in 1888. According to Eighteen-Bisang and Miller [the editors of Stoker's notes for *Dracula*], the practice of using the phonograph to record clinical notations had become common at the time Stoker started to write the novel, and Kittler describes Dr. Seward's phonograph as belonging to a category of 'recently mass produced' technology.*

----

* Leanne Page, 'Phonograph, Shorthand, Typewriter: High Performance Technologies in Bram Stoker's *Dracula*'. Professor Page's informative article can be found online.

Jonathan Harker, a very go-ahead solicitor, is as ahead of the curve in photography as Seward is with phonography. Jonathan takes snaps of likely properties his firm has on its book with his 'Kodak'. He has used the camera to take pictures of Carfax, 'from various points' to show Dracula. Again one reaches out to the 1890s technowhiz:

> A Kodak was an old Victorian handheld camera, so popular that the Eastman Dry Plate Company that created it incorporated it into their name, becoming Eastman Kodak (still around and making cameras today). The Kodak, introduced in 1888, was cheap, compact, and easy to use. It made the previously very complicated process of taking photographs accessible to everyone. Their advertising slogan was: 'You press the button, We do the rest.'*

Young Harker, if he survives his first Romanian client, will go far in the 20th century.

Jonathan keeps his diary in shorthand. We may make a persuasive guess at the notation he uses. The Gregg shorthand system – superior to the clunky old English 'Pitman' – was devised in the late 1880s by John R. Gregg. It inscribed sound, not spelling, as did the earlier Pitman . The phonics were/are (it is still current) cursively transcribed. Gregg could handle phrasing, abbreviated words, and required no lifting of pencil

....
* http://www.bookdrum.com/books/dracula/1128/bookmark/84817.html

from notebook. Above all, it was faster, if harder to learn than Pitman (still being obsoletely taught in British secretarial colleges today).*

John Robert Gregg was born in Northern Ireland. He was considered stupid. It was disability. His hearing had been destroyed by a brutal teacher banging his head. He left school at thirteen. Little was expected of John Gregg. As a copyist of office documents (he had a 'good hand') he was judged too ignorant to learn Pitman. He went on to invent his own, superior, shorthand. It gradually caught on, particularly in America, where new Americans (immigrants) couldn't spell, but could accurately hear phonics.

A wonderful story. His invention was adopted universally in the US, where he emigrated in 1893, and in that year published the manual *Gregg Shorthand*. The system had been available in pamphlets in Britain a year or two earlier. Jonathan, as in other things, was an early adopter.

The faithful Mina (faithful, that is, until Dracula forces his vile fluid exchange on her) types. She has left the classroom, where she taught, to become a 'New Woman', a 'stenographer' – a shorthand typist. It was one of the gateways to female liberation. Women, traditionally dexterous from their sewing, could easily outperform sausage-fingered men on the keyboard. All this is portrayed in Grant Allen's novel *The Typewriter Girl*, published in 1897 (that date again) under the

* My mother, who trained as a shorthand typist after being widowed in the Second World War, used both shorthand systems. I still in handwriting use some Gregg notation picked up from her.

name Olive Pratt Rayner. The technology which liberated such as Mina were the shorthand pad ('take a letter, Miss Murray') and, pre-eminently, the QWERTY typewriter.

Mina is not, however, chained to a clunky desk typewriter. She has what we would call a 'portable', a 'laptop' even. This means she can take the apparatus to Whitby with her, and even to Romania. In the 1890s, Mina's typewriter would be called (as it is in the novel) a 'traveller'. It is tempting to identify her machine as a Columbia portable, which came on to the market in 1885 and weighed only 6lbs. Stoker was, necessarily given the Lyceum theatre's touring, a travelling man. He, it is surmised, may also have used a Columbia to type up *Dracula*.*

Jonathan and Mina will, once combined, make a formidable team. The venerable Exeter solicitors' office, Hawkins and Co., will not know what hit it. The couple are new 20th-century bureaucracy incarnate.

So too is Quincey P. Morris a man of the day, as regards emerging American technology. At one stage in his early thinking about the novel Stoker intended to arm Quincey with a 'Maxim' – the American machine gun. A formidable thought.

In the event Quincey has one of the improved 1894 repeater-action Winchester rifles, with rapid reloading by the lever trigger guard. The '94' would go on to sell by the many million, and become the bestselling civilian-purchasable rifle of all time.

....
* http://www.bookdrum.com/books/dracula/1128/bookmark/200109.html

Quincey proudly totes this fearsome all-American weapon (which, in point of historical fact, was doing more damage to the Native Americans of the Western states than to Romanian vampires).

Finally: in the last, high-action sections of the novel Mina plays a strange role as a receiver and transmitter of mental transmissions from the Count. She is a proto-radio set. The possibilities of this new device had been demonstrated by Nikola Tesla at the 1893 World's Fair in Chicago. Stoker picked it up.

The narrative positively rattles with technological modernity – the modernity of the years 1890–7. Where did Stoker pick it up? Easily answered: from his accompanying Henry Irving on his third (1886) and, particularly, fourth (1893–4) American tours, in which he saw first-hand the techno-revolution which would shape the 20th century. *Dracula* senses it coming.

Dracula:
a chronological plot summary

1 May [1893]: The young lawyer Jonathan Harker leaves Munich for Transylvania via Vienna. He arrives on **3 May** at Bistritz, the nearest town to Castle Dracula with a train connection. He has come to facilitate a property transaction for Count Dracula, who intends to move to London. Dracula instructs him to go by the afternoon coach next day to the Borgo Pass, where he will be met. At nightfall.

After a terrifying drive by horse and carriage through the night, in which the driver does mysterious things, Jonathan is kept waiting at the door of the castle. He is finally offered entry by an old man – the Count – on condition that he enters freely of his own will. Which he does. The castle, Harker discovers, has no other occupants and no servants.

Over the period **5 May–25 June** Jonathan keeps a shorthand diary in which he records that Dracula is sinister and, probably, intends to kill him. Jonathan does not, at this stage, know what vampires are.

He narrowly escapes losing his virginity, and possibly his life, to three 'weird sisters'. An attempt to kill Dracula, lying in his coffin, with a shovel, fails. Finally Jonathan discovers himself alone in the castle. Dracula has left for England, taking Jonathan's clothes and 50 boxes of dirt. Jonathan faces death at the mouths of the three bloodsucking sisters. His diary stops. We know nothing more of him.

9 May: The novel switches back in time to an exchange of letters between Jonathan's fiancée, Mina Murray, and her old school friend, Lucy Westenra. Lucy, just nineteen years old, has received three proposals of marriage: from the asylum keeper, Jack Seward; from the rich American adventurer, Quincey P. Morris; and from the aristocrat Arthur Holmwood. She chooses Holmwood.

25 May: Jack Seward's phonograph diary. He is mortally disappointed by Lucy's rejection.

25 May: Morris writes to Holmwood (an old friend on hunting expeditions), congratulating him. All three men still love Lucy.

25 July–3 August: The story jumps forward to **25 July** and Whitby where Mina and Lucy are spending a holiday together. They have not met since schooldays. Mina befriends a talkative local, Mr Swales. She is worried about not having heard any news from Jonathan.

5 June: Seward describes his strange patient, R.M. Renfield.

3–8 August: A terrible summer storm wrecks a Russian schooner, the *Demeter*, in Whitby Harbour. All on board are dead, the captain's corpse lashed to the wheel. Mysteriously, an 'immense dog' leaps from the wreck to hide itself in the woods behind the town. The captain's log records having left Varna on **6 July**. One by one the crew have been killed in a fog surrounding the ship. The vessel's cargo is wooden boxes of soil.

8–11 August: Mina's journal. Lucy is having mysteriously restless nights' sleep, and sleepwalks. There are small wounds on her neck. A large bat is seen. Mr Swales dies of a broken neck.

17 August: Business correspondence. Boxes, recovered from the *Demeter*, are to be dispatched by railway to London, King's Cross. (There will be one sinister sleeper in the luggage van.)

18 August: Mina's journal. Lucy seems to be recovering. Her nights are now drugged. And so are those of her mother, who has been sleeping in Lucy's bedroom.

19 August: Mina, still in Whitby, receives the joyous news that Jonathan lives, and is being treated in a hospice in Budapest. He has walked hundreds of miles. He remembers nothing of his escape. Mina sets off to Budapest, arriving **24 August**. He gives her his diary to read. Later she will transcribe it to form the first part of the narrative. They marry, on her arrival, in a quiet ceremony.

19 August: Dr Seward notes in his diary that Renfield is strangely disturbed. (He senses the presence of Dracula in nearby Carfax, we suspect.)

24 August: Now in Hillingham, alongside Hampstead Heath, Lucy starts a journal noting that she and her mother are again sleeping badly. Something scrapes against her bedroom window at night.

31 August: Arthur writes to his friend Seward, telling him that the woman they both love, Lucy, looks 'awful'. Something is mysteriously wrong with her.

1 September: Arthur's father, Lord Godalming, is very ill; Arthur must leave Lucy's side to go to him.

2–3 September: Seward writes to Holmwood, still with his dying father, saying that there is nothing organically wrong with Lucy, but she is acutely anaemic. Dangerously so. He has written to an old teacher, Abraham Van Helsing, who might help him. Seward once saved his life. Seward notes continued excitement in his 'zoophagous patient', Renfield.

5–6 September: Seward notes 'terrible change for the worse' in Lucy. He telegrams Van Helsing to come at once, and informs Holmwood by letter. Van Helsing arrives from Holland on **7 September** and immediately prescribes a blood transfusion. Arthur donates. Van Helsing notes a suspicious wound on Lucy's throat.

10 September: Van Helsing protects Lucy's bedroom with garlic and holy paste. Her mother will nurse her at night.

11 September: Lucy describes her going to bed in her diary, ending 'Good night everybody'.

17 September: in her diary Lucy notes improvement. The garlic is working. Renfield cuts Seward's arm and laps up the blood from the floor. A wolf, in Dracula's thrall, escapes from London Zoo and breaks Lucy's window (enabling Dracula to enter). Mrs Westenra dies of fright. Mina sends Lucy a letter (which Lucy will be too weak to open when it arrives). She and Jonathan are back in England.

18 September: Seward arrives at Hillingham to discover a crisis in Lucy's condition. Morris appears, sent by Holmwood. He donates blood – her fourth transfusion (Seward and Van Helsing also having donated in the intervening days). Mr Hawkins dies, leaving Jonathan in charge of the Exeter firm.

20 September: Renfield attacks the coach which he mysteriously knows is moving his master from Carfax to London. Lucy has died, as has Holmwood's father. Arthur is now Lord Godalming and he is free to claim Lucy in Hillingham. She expires, a vampire. Arthur cannot even – as Van Helsing warns – kiss her farewell.

21 September: The funeral and burial of Lucy and her mother. Van Helsing tells Seward that Lucy's corpse, once interred, must be de-vampirised.

22 September: Arthur and Quincey P. Morris renew their friendship. Mina and the convalescent Jonathan travel to Exeter for Mr Hawkins's funeral.

23 September: Jonathan catches sight of Dracula in Hyde Park. He has 'grown young'.

25 September: The *Westminster Gazette* reports children being mysteriously abducted and injured at night on Hampstead Heath by a 'bloofer lady'.

23–24 September: Mina's Journal. Jonathan continues

to recover. Van Helsing writes to warn her that something terrible must be done. She telegrams him to come immediately. She has read Jonathan's journal.

25 September: In her journal Mina records meeting Van Helsing. He reads Jonathan's diary. All is becoming clear.

26 September: Jonathan is strong enough to take up his diary again. He and Van Helsing discuss the Count. In his phonograph diary Seward records conversations with the Dutchman and the mysterious business of the children on Hampstead Heath. 'They were made by Miss Lucy,' Van Helsing says. Action must be taken. Van Helsing and Seward go to Lucy's tomb by night and open the coffin at St John-at-Hampstead graveyard. It is empty. They save a child from her vampire clutches.

27 September: The two men repeat the visit. The tomb is now again occupied by Lucy: 'radiantly beautiful' – from the blood of local children. Van Helsing stands watch at the graveyard.

28 September: Arthur, Quincey, Seward and Van Helsing make a night-time expedition to the graveyard. Lucy is roaming. When she returns, Arthur is persuaded to drive a stake through her heart; whereupon she is again pure Lucy Westenra (albeit dead).

29–30 September: Seward allows Mina to hear his diary cylinders. She will type them out, making carbon copies. The four men and she are now united in their aim to hunt down Dracula. Or is he hunting them? Seward now realises that the estate next door has been the vampire's lair and that Renfield has some close connection with Dracula. Jonathan goes to London to track 'Count de Ville's' lodgings in the city.

30 September: Mina's journal. She finishes her copying and consoles the distraught Holmwood. She meets Renfield, who behaves with extraordinary courtesy. He seems to fall in love with her. In Seward's office, Van Helsing explains what vampires really are.

1 October: Seward's journal. Renfield implores that he be released from the asylum. His mood is volatile and fearful. Harker describes a raid on Carfax. The Count is not there. Jonathan notices that Mina is looking strangely pale. Mina's diary records her feeling weak. Something seems to have been trying to get into her bedroom. Jonathan leaves her at home. He is making progress, as his diary records, in tracking down Dracula in London.

2 October: Seward posts a guard on Renfield's room. On the following day, **3 October**, he is found mortally injured. Van Helsing is called and manages to question him. He explains, at length, how Dracula took control of him and has been visiting him as a mist. The men go to Mina's room and see Dracula. He has been drinking her blood, and forcing her to drink his. He escapes Quincey, who goes out to look for him in the woods.

3 October: Harker's journal. Renfield's burial. The vampire hunters mobilise. Van Helsing puts a crucifix on Mina's forehead. It scorches and leaves a terrible scar.

3–4 October: Seward's diary. Dracula has escaped Morris in London. Van Helsing hypnotises Mina. Via her mental link with the vampire they discover that, with only one box of earth left, Dracula intends to embark to some port in Europe; thence, presumably, to the safety of his castle. Van Helsing leaves a message on Seward's phonograph that he will try to catch Dracula before the sun goes down. He fails.

5 October: Mina appoints herself the recorder of what is to come. They track down the vessel on which Dracula has left, the *Czarina Catherine*. Jonathan discovers that his wife is subject to the Count's will.

11 October: Seward describes the contact between Mina and Dracula: she is free of the Count's influence only at sunrise and sunset. The men are resolved to save her – or, if not her, her soul.

15–27 October: the party board a cross-channel train as the first step of their pursuit. Under hypnosis, Mina describes Dracula on his sea voyage – but where to? Harker and Seward record events: Seward longs for his phonograph. They wait in the port of Varna.

28–30 October: Dracula's port of entry has been located. But is Dracula using Mina to mislead them? It is not at Varna he arrives, but at Galatz. They go there but Dracula has again eluded them. They have a council of war. Despite her condition Mina is faithfully recording everything. She is protected by sleeping in a 'holy circle', fashioned by Van Helsing.

31 October–4 November: They have reached Bistritz and are closing in on Dracula, the last stage by horse.

6 November: Mina's journal. They finally engage Dracula and his gypsy guard at sunset. Mina and Van Helsing are observing from a safe distance. In the nick of time, the men kill Dracula. Morris, who deals the vampire a fatal blow, is mortally injured. Dracula dissolves into dust. The scar disappears from Mina's brow.

1900: Jonathan pens an epilogue. He and Mina have a child, Quincey. They have made a summer trip to Transylvania. Godalming is 'happily married', as is Seward. Van Helsing lives on.

What happened in Munich?

～※～

Munich is mentioned only once in the published novel – in the opening sentence, which could have been discharged, rat-a-tat from Quincey's Maxim machine gun.

> *3 May. Bistritz.* – Left Munich at 8.35 P.M., on 1st May, arriving at Vienna early next morning; should have arrived at 6.46, but train was an hour late.

Quincey's Maxim gun was erased from the printed text.

Also erased, one can plausibly speculate, was what looks, to the thoughtful eye, like a substantial prequel to the published *Dracula*, set in Munich.

The Munich prelude would have tied up some hanging threads in the narrative as published. But in the interests of pace, Stoker decided to let the threads hang and get on with the story. There remain nonetheless wisps of plot-thought in the surviving notes which enable one plausibly to construct what that prequel to Jonathan's departure from Munich might have been.

In large outline, it seems that: (a) Harker was conceived as having been in the Bavarian city as a tourist in transit enjoying a stopover for three or four days; (b) Dracula was coincidentally, or by design, in Munich at the same time. Tourism was not in prospect. Perhaps he was in this German financial centre because of his need for ready cash in a negotiable currency, as I surmise elsewhere (see page 164). Something more complex, that is, than could be achieved by local Bistritz bureaux de change, if indeed there were such things.

The surviving memoranda enable one to put some flesh on this lost Munich episode. It is, incidentally, set in freezing snowy winter, not May. Stoker made that seasonal change to early summer presumably to fit in with the eve of St George's Day, 4 May.

What one can reasonably reconstruct from the tantalisingly brief surviving notes is as follows. There was, the first note records, a telegram from Dracula to Hawkins, in Exeter, to start for Munich. Dracula expected his 'good friend' Hawkins to come himself.

The urgency of a telegram could suggest that Dracula himself was in the German city, or expecting to be there imminently. Again, it is hard to imagine him sending telegrams from any convenient postal office in the environs of Castle Dracula.

For what is called in the notes 'Chapter 2' there is some elaboration. What Dracula now sends is a letter, not a telegram. The letter contains instructions that Harker, Hawkins's substitute, should stay at Munich's Auracher Hof[f] hotel, and await instructions. The hotel, a first-rate establishment, still exists. Over the next few days Harker, awaiting further instruction, entertains himself with a visit to the Pinnacothek [*sic*; i.e. 'picture'] gallery and a night at the opera. There he sees *The Flying Dutchman*, by Richard Wagner, whose cursed, immortal hero has clear connections with his future host.*

Of even more prophetic significance to Harker, however, is the city's 'waiting house' or *Leichenhaus* (literally, 'corpse house') – a public mortuary. Munich had an unusual burial law. Anyone dying within city limits was obliged to lie, in public view, in the *Leichenhaus* alongside the municipal cemetery for three days. The aim was ostensibly to prevent premature burial – a 19th-century phobia. The Catholic superstition about not sleeping under the same roof as a dead person was another factor. As a commentator notes:

> Müncheners regard going to the Deadhouse on holidays as a standard recreation, and always recommend it to visitors with a weird sort of pride. They go through life perfectly unconcerned over the prospect that some day they, too, will be taken there to lie in lowly state for three days before the clods of the grave close over them.†

The bodies were laid out on display, in open coffins, covered by cloth. The coffins were surrounded by flowers to obliterate any stench of decomposition. The temperature in the corpse house was kept warm, to speed up decomposition as proof of death.

* Stoker took over management of Irving's Lyceum Theatre in 1878. The first production he took charge of was *Vanderdecken*, David Belasco's take on the tale of the Flying Dutchman.

† http://hauntedohiobooks.com/news/munich-dead-house. It is quoted and discussed by Skal.

In the house of the dead Harker sees an old man laid out on a bier. On a visit the next day he overhears some conversation. The old man's body has mysteriously disappeared. Where? Who would steal such a thing?

'Harker has seen the corpse but does not take part in discussion'. The face on that corpse will, later, be significant to him when he meets Dracula. They are one and the same. He returns to the Auruch to wait. In the morning he receives a wire ('~~letter~~' is crossed out in the notes) from Transylvania. He is to make haste and travel on to Bistritz and there remain until he is collected.

One can put the parts together like so much narrative Lego. Dracula was in Munich on some unspecified necessary business. He, of course, is the old man who disappears from the corpse house. It has been convenient to him (given that the ground is consecrated) to use the place as his hostelry. He came and went to Munich by coffin, handled by his loyal gypsy crew.

The distance between Munich and Bistritz is 800 miles. The larger part of Dracula's encoffined journey would have been undertaken in the luggage wagons of trains. He will arrive at his castle shortly before Jonathan. At that point, the published novel takes off, with Jonathan leaving Munich.

In terms of narrative tactics the erasure of the Munich prequel was wise. It would have been cumbersome and Stoker's novel was turning out to be too long. But the dropping of the episode probably nagged at Stoker. He knew Germany, and Munich, from Henry Irving's 1882 tour to the country, which he had managed. He did not know Transylvania. He must have felt a certain guilt – as if he were, somehow, fooling his readers and borrowing too much from Emily Gerard.

The dropped Munich episode left a puzzling relic. In 1914 Florence Stoker, in a makeweight collection of Bram's short 'weird' stories, included a piece entitled *Dracula's Guest*.

It is clearly disconnected notes rather than a short story and may have been fleshed out for publication by another hand than Stoker's. Florence added in her preface the explanation:

> To his original list of stories in this book, I have added an hitherto unpublished episode from *Dracula*. It was originally excised owing to the length of the book, and may prove of interest to the many readers of what is considered my husband's most remarkable work.

Indeed it does prove of interest, with reference to both the published novel and the unpublished Munich episode. 'Dracula's Guest' occupies the first place in the volume.

A young unnamed Englishman stops over in Munich *en route* to Transylvania at the Quatre Saisons Hotel. It is Walpurgisnacht in Germany. April 30th. All hell will be let loose. The hero does not speak German and has not the faintest idea of what this sinister night holds for him.

Relishing the 'early summer' air, he goes for an afternoon drive in a carriage. Ignoring the hotel manager's instruction that he must be back before nightfall, he decides to go on a moonlight ramble. By foot. Inadvisable. His driver, Johann, who has been consulting his watch every few minutes, gallops off at twilight in a spirit of every man for himself. The maddened horses are of the same view. Leave the mad Englishman to the witches.

The hero takes in the views touristically as the sun goes down. But the temperature suddenly drops as well. He hears a wolf howl. Then a veritable blizzard begins to blow:

> As I looked there came a cold shiver in the air, and the snow began to fall. I thought of the miles and miles of bleak country I had passed, and then hurried on to seek the shelter of the wood in front. Darker and darker grew the sky, and faster and heavier fell the snow, till the earth before and around me was a glistening white carpet the further edge of which was lost in misty vagueness.

The odd gleam of moonlight penetrates the swirling black clouds. The narrator-hero discovers he is in a graveyard. There is a chorus of wolf howls. He sees a large tomb and approaches it for shelter:

> Then while the flood of moonlight still fell on the marble tomb, the storm gave further evidence of renewing, as though it was returning on its track. Impelled by some sort of fascination, I approached the sepulchre to see what it was, and why such a thing stood alone in such a place. I walked around it, and read, over the Doric door, in German:

COUNTESS DOLINGEN OF GRATZ
IN STYRIA SOUGHT AND FOUND DEATH
1801

On the top of the tomb, seemingly driven through the solid marble – for the structure was composed of a few vast blocks of stone – was a great iron spike or stake. On going to the back I saw, graven in great Russian letters:

> 'The dead travel fast.'

The hero has no idea what it means.

Stoker's first intention was to set his narrative, like Le Fanu's lesbian-vampire fable *Carmilla*, in Styria (Austria). A connection of some kind between the woman interred here and the heroines – one vampire, one victim in Le Fanu's novel – is suggested.* No more than that. Suicides and vampires were customarily staked in their graves – less flamboyantly than my lady Dolingen. 'The dead travel fast', a quote from Gottfried Bürger's poem 'Lenore', with its vampire theme, is echoed by one of the passengers in the coach which drops off Jonathan Harker at the Borgo Pass in *Dracula*. What is implied by the Countess seeking and finding death is not spelled out. An unwritten novel lies in the inscription.

There follows a 'perfect tornado'. Hail falls in a violent cascade and the hero is forced to take shelter deeper in the tomb. He thinks he sees something inexplicable:

....
* See the summary of *Carmilla* on pages 43–5.

> as I am a living man, I saw, as my eyes were turned
> into the darkness of the tomb, a beautiful woman,
> with rounded cheeks and red lips, seemingly sleeping
> on a bier.

He senses there is someone living, or, worse, not living, alongside him. Lightning strikes the iron stake pinning down the Countess; she rises screaming. The hero faints, as well he might. He half wakes to feel something (some 'thing') warmly 'rasping' at his throat. When he dares look, he sees it is a gigantic wolf lying on him. He is being raped by the beast.

He is rescued, in the nick of time, by a troop of soldiers: werewolf hunters. They frighten off his furry assailant and take him back to the hotel. The manager has received a telegram from Dracula. It instructs him to take particular care of this guest. Dracula has need of the young man undamaged. He is to leave for Bistritz post-haste.

One rather wishes that Stoker could have found a way of incorporating this vivid episode in his published text.

Why is Stoker's vampire aristocratic?

༄༅

It's odd. The image of the vampire before Stoker historically is typically of some low-born corpse who won't lie still in his shallow grave. Proletarian at best, more often a peasant. Dracula is something else. He is a count to the tip of his unnaturally long and pointed fingernails. Well-bred.

Romania, people who know about such things remind us, doesn't have 'counts'. It is, so spelled, a distinctly English honour. Dracula, in his own country, would be a *boyar*. That word appears four times in the text. 'Count' appears 237 times.

There is a patina of British aristocracy layered over the Romanian vampire. Whence comes it? The question leads back to the most famed and notorious (if one excepts the Earl of Rochester) aristocrat in British Literature: George Gordon Lord Byron. It's connected via that name to a backstory which takes us into the Regency literary world. The story is well known – novels and TV dramas have been written about it – but it merits retelling.

The unprecedentedly wet summer of 1816 and the inconvenience it caused a party of distinguished literary tourists

– Lord Byron, Percy Shelley, Mary Godwin, Claire Clairmont and John Polidori, Byron's attendant doctor – is legendary. Climatically, the bad weather began far away in Indonesia, with the eruption of Mount Tambora. It hit seven on the Volcanic Explosivity Index, making it the largest such event in a thousand years. The result, worldwide, was the 'year without a summer' and a (less deadly) eruption of Gothicism in Villa Diodati, alongside Lake Geneva, where the English *littérateurs* were staying. Pent up by the foul weather, they beguiled the rainy days and nights with a competition to write the most spine-chilling ghost story their highly creative minds could come up with.

Mary Godwin (soon to be Mary Shelley) was evidently struck by the fact that Milton had once resided in Villa Diodati. She elected to rewrite *Paradise Lost* as *Frankenstein*. Shelley and Byron rather fizzled out: literature was, in the final analysis, more than a parlour game for them. Nonetheless, as a striking entry in Polidori's diary testifies, they remained receptive listeners:

L[ord] B[yron] repeated some verses of Coleridge's *Christabel*, of the witch's breast; when silence ensued, and Shelley, suddenly shrieking and putting his hands to his head, ran out of the room with a candle. Threw water on his face, and after gave him ether. He was looking at Mrs S[helley], and suddenly thought of a woman he had heard of who had eyes instead of nipples, which, taking hold of his mind, horrified him.

Polidori was, like the eighteen-year-old Mary, young – in his case, barely twenty. The two of them got on well. A graduate of Edinburgh Medical School (the youngest ever to qualify, supposedly), Polidori had learned his sawbone trade (which he despised) on cadavers supplied by Edinburgh's famous so-called 'resurrectionists' – a grim joke. Medical science needed corpses: the supply from the gallows and the stillborn (the only legitimate sources) was inadequate. Neither would rotting cadavers do. Anatomists needed 'fresh meat', still warm, ideally. Burke and Hare, the most notorious of the resurrectionists, solved the supply problem by murder.

Polidori had written his thesis on 'somnambulism'. He was fascinated by the paranormal. A second-generation Italo-Englishman, he was handsome, politically radical, and a vibrant (if rather too interruptive) conversationalist.

Polidori had found himself at the Villa Diodati by a once-in-a-lifetime stroke of luck. Byron, immersed in sexual scandal, had decided that England was too hot for him. He would decamp, and he needed a travelling companion – preferably a physician. Byron was taken with Polidori, whom he had met socially. The young man was recruited for the duration of the tour abroad, on a handsome stipend of £500.

Polidori was flattered to the point of intoxication. Byron's closest friend, John Cam Hobhouse, loathed 'Polly-Wolly' and sowed as much distrust as he could. It was unnecessary. The young medic soon got on Byron's nerves and things were not helped by 'The Vampyre', the tale Polly came up with in their ghost story competition. Clearly the hero of that short tale, Lord Ruthven, is a version of Byron.

Intended as flattery, Polidori's story was tactless and clumsy. The plot of 'The Vampyre' is simple. The sinister Lord Ruthven* takes the handsome young Aubrey on a continental tour with him. On his travels, Ruthven cold-bloodedly destroys every young person who comes his way. Finally, having sucked Aubrey dry, he turns his dead, grey, irresistible eye on Aubrey's sister:

> Aubrey's weakness increased; the effusion of blood produced symptoms of the near approach of death. He desired his sister's guardians might be called, and when the midnight hour had struck ... he died immediately after. The guardians hastened to protect Miss Aubrey; but when they arrived, it was too late. Lord Ruthven had disappeared, and Aubrey's sister had glutted the thirst of a VAMPYRE!

No need to call for the ether. One's spine is obstinately unchilled. Shortly after reading this Byron kicked Polidori out, sending him across the Alps alone, friendless and penniless. On his return to England, Polidori drifted, gambled wildly, and suffered a disastrous head injury in a coach accident in 1818, which exacerbated a temperamental disposition towards melancholy.

....

* The pseudonym Lady Caroline Lamb had applied to her thinly disguised Byronic villain-hero in her roman-à-clef *Glenarvon*.

'The Vampyre' went into oblivion. Until that is, the rascally publisher Henry Colburn came on the scene. Colburn was infatuated with Byron and all things Byronic. Virtually every copy of his magazine the *New Monthly* contained something connected with the mad, bad lord – the most celebrated of Regency celebrities. Colburn duly arranged the publication of 'The Vampyre: A tale related by Lord Byron to John Polidori' in his magazine. Later, with some modification, it was published in booklet form, again purportedly as a tale by Byron, transcribed by Polidori.

I discuss the chicanery and jiggery-pokery of this sorry episode elsewhere.* But, briefly, late in the day clarifications came after Colburn had made a mint of money and fended off lawsuits. The reading public did not care about intricacies of authorship.

On its publication 'The Vampyre' was universally taken to be a shameless self-portrait by the world's most ruthless womaniser (a founder member of the 'League of Incest'). With Byron's name attached to it, or dragged behind it, the 'trashy tale' was sensationally popular. Five book editions came out in 1819 alone. There were translations (pirated) in Europe, dramatic adaptations, and an opera. There was nothing new about vampires as such, but the literary effect of 'The Vampyre' was momentous. It not only inspired but forever 'Byronised' the genre. Polidori died aged 25 in 1821,

---

* In *Lives of the Novelists* (2011).

suicidally depressed, and probably by a self-administered dose of prussic acid.

The 'Vampyre' affair was a murky business: But it left a consequence. The aristocratic vampire. This idea was picked up by Thomas Preskett Prest, taking the form of Sir Francis Varney in *Varney the Vampire; or, the Feast of Blood*. It was a penny serial for the masses. But the notable fact is that the hero is a blood-sucking, vampiric aristocrat. A 'trope' was founded.

Who invented the Dracula tux?

❧

Dracula's sartorial standards are not, as Stoker portrays them, high. In one of the meaner of his acts, for example, he steals Harker's clothes before going off on his epic jaunt to England. The notion of the enemy of mankind doing his worst in a stolen pair of solicitor's clerk's trousers is a bit of a comedown.

Dracula wears, when the choice is his, an all-black outfit. His look. But white gloves and a straw hat are mentioned by workers at Doolittle's Wharf, where his boxes are being transported. Elsewhere, the zookeeper recalls:

> '... There wasn't much people about that day, and close at hand was only one man, a tall, thin chap, with a 'ook nose and a pointed beard, with a few white hairs runnin' through it. He had a 'ard, cold look and red eyes, and I took a sort of mislike to him, for it seemed as if it was 'im as they was hirritated at. He 'ad white kid gloves on 'is 'ands, and he pointed out the animiles to me and says: "Keeper, these wolves seem upset at something." ...'

As regards the straw hat, Van Helsing – not a connoisseur of dress – observes, 'it suits not him'. One can't see Christopher Lee going with it.

Wardrobe became a critical issue with stage and film versioning. Max Schreck in the primal film *Nosferatu* simply went for East European drab. But Dracula is a count, even if he can hardly be said always to have noble blood in his veins. One wonders about how faddy he is. In Transylvania he leaves the peasant woman to the wolves and throws her babe to his harem. In England the only victims we see him interested in are the eminently upper-class Mina and Lucy.

We associate Dracula with a certain mode of dress: essentially the dark dandyism pioneered by the novelist and politician Edward Bulwer-Lytton in the 1830s, as a revolt against Beau Brummelism.* The well-dressed Victorian gent clothed himself as if going to a funeral. 'Charcoal grey' was the gayest colour.

On stage the dark-dandy Dracula originates in 1924, with Hamilton Deane's theatrical version. It was the first production to receive Florence Stoker's assent and she granted the privilege partly as a protest against the grimy *Nosferatu* travesty, as she saw it (see page 59). Dracula should embody at least the outward quality of British gentlemanliness. Rephrase that as *English* gentlemanliness. He should be dressed adequately for the Windham gentlemen's club.

Renfield, before he took to the straitjacket, was a member of the Windham, as was Arthur's father, Lord Holmwood. So too were Sir Henry Irving and his assistant, Mr Stoker. If it

* That is, the colourful garb popularised – for those who could afford it – by the Prince Regent's (and Byron's) particular friend Beau Brummel, virtuoso of the cravat.

were just a question of external appearance they could have proposed Deane's version of Count Dracula for membership, no questions asked.

Playing the Count on stage, Raymond Huntley drew on his own wardrobe, allegedly, to create a Dracula who could, in appearance, quite easily have ambled into a Noel Coward drawing room comedy. Deane, in the supporting role of Van Helsing, was similarly well turned out. It was gent versus gent to the death.

The production toured for years until Huntley was fed up to the false canines with it. He felt trapped in a role which was beneath his talent. But he had been instrumental in creating an image of Count Dracula which is still with us.*

The black-tie dinner jacket – 'tux' in American parlance – became fashionable by its association with Dracula. Hamilton Deane took his *Dracula* to Broadway in 1927, Bela Lugosi replacing the fed-up Huntley and thereafter going on to star in the 1931 Tod Browning movie. Deane did the scenario. Bela Lugosi was duly tuxified, with an odd medallion hanging round his neck which has been an object of fascinated speculation among Dracula enthusiasts.

American teenaged youth, a genus which rarely dresses for dinner, revels in the Dracula tux every Halloween. On that night in November, the Count 'lives' again.

---

* See http://www.smithsonianmag.com/arts-culture/why-does-dracula-wear-a-tuxedo-the-origins-of-bram-stokers-timeless-vampire-101868474/ #rZoSZKLSSfwCsjot.99. Huntley went on to do good work in film.

How rich is Dracula?

༚༚

A t the period Stoker was writing *Dracula*, 1890 until May 1897, H.G. Wells was writing a novel, originally intended to be published simultaneously. It was called *The Sleeper Wakes*.

Wells, fearing Victoria's Diamond Jubilee would distract England from his book, withheld *The Sleeper Wakes* until 1898. The novel's early sections are set in 1897, its futuristic sections in 2001. It would have been pleasing if Stoker's and Wells's novels had come out cheek by jowl. There is a fascinating conjunction of theme.

Wells's 'sleeper' – Graham by name, a lone wolf by nature – falls into a deep sleep. Science cannot wake him, but it can preserve his body. Blood transfusions keep Graham going for two centuries. The procedure – the infusion of life into another body – was beginning to be successfully practised at Edinburgh in the early 1890s but not rendered entirely safe until 1901, when blood types were identified.* Had he survived into the 20th century, Dracula could have saved himself, and humankind, a lot of trouble by raiding hospital blood refrigerators.

....
* Lucy was as likely to be killed by a disparity of blood types among her four donors as by Dracula.

Graham wakes, in 2001, to find that by the miracle of compound interest he now owns all the wealth in the world. He is king, boss, master.

Dracula has potentially had many more centuries to accumulate wealth than Graham. And he is very interested in ready money. Hence his laborious expeditions with spade over his shoulder on St George's Night (see below, 'Why is Dracula so interested in blue flames?', page 159). It's the only work, other than some bedmaking, we see him do.

Dracula's money is in very old gold. Harker sees a mountain of it in the castle treasure room. It is very valuable and growing ever more so. There was anxiety in the 1890s that the world's supply of the precious metal was running out. Hence the British Empire's willingness to fight a war for the possession of South African gold mines.

How rich, then, is Dracula? If he can buy 50 houses in London he is manifestly an extremely well-heeled vampire. Right at the top of the 1893 international rich list. Wells's scientific romance is a young socialist's parable about accumulative capitalism and the tyrannies it spawns. It is worth spending a little time thinking about Dracula's very different econo-politico-socio subtext.*

The ever-illuminating Franco Moretti sees Stoker's novel as fuelled by 1890s panic about foreign money flooding into

----

* I am indebted here to Jasmine Yong Hall, 'Solicitors Soliciting: The Dangerous Circulations of Professionalism in *Dracula*', in *The New Nineteenth Century: Feminist Readings of Unread Victorian Fiction*, eds Barbara Leah Harman and Susan Meyer (1999).

Britain, sucking away its national selfhood. Assimilation is never in prospect on Dracula's part. He sleeps on his own, consecrated, foreign soil. Fifty boxes of the stuff. He uses England. He has not the slightest intention of becoming English. Leave that to the serfs.

Dracula, the oligarch vampire, can be aligned with vulgar depictions of, for example, the Rothschilds. Stoker played down any anti-Semitism in the novel (the first word in his notes, 'Aaronson', is erased and replaced with the gentile 'Hawkins'). As a man of the London theatre, a traditionally philo-Semitic world, Stoker was never that way inclined. Nor was he carried away by the British anti-Jewish panic, as Russian pogroms drove multitudes of desperate Jews to seek last-hope refuge in the US and UK. But, nonetheless, there is a touch of 1890s anti-Semitic prejudice in at least one point of the novel (see 'How much German does Jonathan speak?', page 69). It does no damage but one wishes it wasn't there.

Dracula's wealth is literally torn from the body of Romania, drenched as it has been in history by blood and treasure. Dracula loves his blood- and gold-enriched native dirt. As he explains to a wondering Jonathan, who has witnessed him digging up gold from the tell-tale blue flames:

'That treasure has been hidden ... in the region through which you came last night, there can be but little doubt; for it was the ground fought over for centuries by the Wallachian, the Saxon, and the Turk. Why, there is hardly a foot of soil in all this region that

has not been enriched by the blood of men, patriots
or invaders.'

In the past, Dracula says, the population would bury their
wealth to protect it from the invading hordes. Why, inquires
Jonathan, hasn't it been dug up since? The Count smiles:
'Because your peasant is at heart a coward and a fool!'

Gold, where geological forces have created it, is found in
dirt and so is Dracula's. The difference being that his gold is
crusted in blood. And history. How rich a vampire is he? The
richest.

Why won't Dracula
let Jonathan go home?

～※～

Early in the action, Jonathan Harker asks himself a very pertinent question, as he stands outside the door of Castle Dracula, waiting forever, it seems, for it to swing open on its rusty hinges:

> I stood in silence where I was, for I did not know what to do. Of bell or knocker there was no sign; through these frowning walls and dark window openings it was not likely that my voice could penetrate. The time I waited seemed endless, and I felt doubts and fears crowding upon me. What sort of place had I come to, and among what kind of people? What sort of grim adventure was it on which I had embarked? Was this a customary incident in the life of a solicitor's clerk sent out to explain the purchase of a London estate to a foreigner?

An Exeter solicitor, to boot. This is turning out to be the worst holiday in Jonathan's short life.

Why has Dracula demanded a clerk be sent him? Originally,

of course, it was to be Mr Hawkins who came over to see the client who promised his firm rich pickings. But Mr Hawkins has contracted a strategic (we may assume) attack of gout. He does not appear in the novel. I like to fantasise that he has made some inquiries and come up with some worrying answers. Dracula (see below) refers to Hawkins as 'my friend'. That word, in that mouth, has a sinister ring to it. Hawkins dies shortly after Dracula arrives in England. Payback?

Whatever the reason, young Harker is shipped off to Transylvania. A promotion to partnership soothes any resentment. His marriage to Mina can wait.

The reason for Dracula's demanding the presence of an English clerk and his reluctance thereafter to release him can be guessed at, although Stoker, for his own narrative purposes, keeps it shrouded in foggy mystery. It is not, we deduce, because Count Dracula wants to 'vamp' Jonathan. Male necks are not to his taste – despite Renfield's mad hopes that he will get the immortalising kiss.

The fact is that the Count needs Jonathan as a source of instruction as to how to behave in England. Dracula has never, apparently, met, or, perish the thought, impaled, an Englishman.* He has picked up the language from books. His command of the tongue is excellent, Jonathan tells him. The Count declines the compliment.

....

* He *may*, as I have argued elsewhere, have three English ladies in his vaults (see pages 34–5), which would help with the language, but not with the finer points of English gentlemanly behaviour.

'I thank you, my friend, for your all too-flattering esti-
mate, but yet I fear that I am but a little way on the
road I would travel. True, I know the grammar and
the words, but yet I know not how to speak them.'

He fears he will cut a poor figure in the teeming streets and
drawing rooms of the world's premier city. Worse even than
that, he will be laughed at. Intolerable. His pride could not
stand such a thing. He needs Jonathan not as a clerk, but a
tutor:

'Well, I know that, did I move and speak in your
London, none there are who would not know me for
a stranger. That is not enough for me. Here I am noble;
I am *boyar*; the common people know me, and I am
master. But a stranger in a strange land, he is no one;
men know him not – and to know not is to care not
for. I am content if I am like the rest, so that no man
stops if he see me, or pause in his speaking if he hear
my words, to say "Ha, ha! a stranger!" I have been so
long master that I would be master still – or at least
that none other should be master of me. You come to
me not alone as agent of my friend Peter Hawkins, of
Exeter, to tell me all about my new estate in London.
You shall, I trust, rest here with me awhile, so that by
our talking I may learn the English intonation; and I
would that you tell me when I make error, even of the
smallest, in my speaking. I am sorry that I had to be

away so long to-day; but you will, I know, forgive one
who has so many important affairs in hand.'

When finally, after six weeks' foretaste of hell for his unwilling
guest, Dracula takes off for his London adventure, he pinches
Jonathan's suit, overcoat and travelling rug. But the solicitor's
clerk has given him more than clothing. He has helped the
Count *English* himself. Beware Piccadilly.

Whose face does
Jonathan remember?

಄಄

There is an enigmatic sentence in Jonathan's recollection of his near-violation by the three sisters:

> They came close to me, and looked at me for some time, and then whispered together. Two were dark [...]
> The other was fair, as fair as can be, with great wavy masses of golden hair and eyes like pale sapphires. *I seemed somehow to know her face, and to know it in connection with some dreamy fear, but I could not recollect at the moment how or where.* [my italics]

The fair sister is urged by her dark comrades to have the first 'kiss', so-called. They repeat the word 'kiss' – it is not, we apprehend, a friendly peck they are thinking of.

It is strange. In the civilised world Jonathan comes from, women do not initiate the lover's kiss, lunging like hungry piranha at the male's face. Leave that to the mythical harpy (who actually preferred tearing out men's livers). 'Ladies' would receive the chosen one's proffered lips demurely. Sometimes with faux reluctance, averting the head so that the female cheek receives the male mouth.

It has been suggested that what Jonathan is 'dreamily' remembering here is his experience with the un-dead Countess Dolingen, in the dropped Munich prelude (published, long after the novel, as 'Dracula's Guest' – see 'What Happened in Munich?', page 108). The suggestion has plausibility. But Stoker leaves it open enough that there is opportunity for some other, equally plausible guesses.

Are these women all that is left of what was once a whole community inhabiting the castle? One's mind shifts to one of the most memorable passages in the novel. Jonathan, exploring the vast building in which he now knows he is imprisoned, comes across a new part of it:

> From the windows I could see that the suite of rooms lay along to the south of the castle, the windows of the end room looking out both west and south. On the latter side, as well as to the former, there was a great precipice. The castle was built on the corner of a great rock, so that on three sides it was quite impregnable, and great windows were placed here where sling, or bow, or culverin could not reach, and consequently light and comfort, impossible to a position which had to be guarded, were secured. To the west was a great valley, and then, rising far away, great jagged mountain fastnesses, rising peak on peak, the sheer rock studded with mountain ash and thorn, whose roots clung in cracks and crevices and crannies of the stone. This was evidently the portion of the castle

occupied by the ladies in bygone days, for the furniture had more air of comfort than any I had seen. The windows were curtainless, and the yellow moonlight, flooding in through the diamond panes, enabled one to see even colours, whilst it softened the wealth of dust which lay over all and disguised in some measure the ravages of time and the moth. My lamp seemed to be of little effect in the brilliant moonlight, but I was glad to have it with me, for there was a dread loneliness in the place which chilled my heart and made my nerves tremble. Still, it was better than living alone in the rooms which I had come to hate from the presence of the Count, and after trying a little to school my nerves, I found a soft quietude come over me. Here I am, sitting at a little oak table where in old times possibly some fair lady sat to pen, with much thought and many blushes, her ill-spelt love-letter, and writing in my diary in shorthand all that has happened since I closed it last. It is nineteenth century up-to-date with a vengeance. And yet, unless my senses deceive me, the old centuries had, and have, powers of their own which mere 'modernity' cannot kill.

The clash of ages, antiquity and modernity, which is at the heart of the novel's thinking, is articulated authoritatively here with a burst of Stoker's finest descriptive prose.

But various puzzles remain: how has Dracula become sole master and inhabitant of this castle, which once teemed with the complicated clan household of a local medieval ruler and military commanders? That we shall never know.

The 'fair lady' clearly evokes Mina – who is, at this moment, in another country, practising her 'new woman' office skills. The 'fair one' in Castle Dracula is, one suspects, not 'new': any more than la belle dame sans merci is new. She is as old as myth itself.

The spirit of her age, summer 1893, allows Mina to flex her 'man's brain' in ways her women ancestors never could. But she is also described (repeatedly by Van Helsing) as 'angelic': a genus traditionally fair-haired in Victorian social myth, submissive to male will, and ultra-female. One thinks of the poem (beloved in its time) 'The Angel in the House', by Coventry Patmore. Then, as now, a 'real' man would never be described as 'angelic'.

When we last get a sense of her, in the narrative's epilogue, Mrs Harker is no new woman, but a model wife and mother cut from traditional cloth. An angel in Jonathan Harker's house. Victorians saw it, most of them, as a happy ending. We, perhaps, do not.

What seems the most likely reading to me as the fair lady's lips come towards Jonathan is his evaporating fidelity to Mina. He suddenly wants demons, not angels. The 'other', when it comes to sex, is more seductive and more dangerous. It always is. Ask men through the ages.

The Victorians, we conclude, loaded much more significance into the concept of the kiss than we do. It was the sole sexual contact permitted premarital lovers, if they were following approved social codes. The period's ideology of osculation (so to call it) was raised to iconic status by one of its most famous paintings, Dante Gabriel Rossetti's *Bocca Baciata* ('The Kissed Mouth'). The portrait is a tribute to the 'bee-stung lips' of the painter's mistress, Fanny Cornforth. The painting carries a motto, in Italian: *Bocca baciata non perde ventura, anzi rinnova come fa la luna* ('The mouth that has been kissed does not lose its savour, indeed it renews itself just as the moon does').

As Wikipedia* usefully informs us:

> Rossetti, an accomplished translator of early Italian literature, probably knew the proverb from Boccaccio's *Decameron* where it is used as the culmination of the tale of Alatiel: a beautiful Saracen princess who, despite having had sex on perhaps ten thousand occasions with eight separate lovers in the space of four years, successfully presents herself to the King of the Algarve as his virgin bride.

Kathryn Hughes, who has most recently analysed Rossetti's painting,[†] reminds us that Cornforth, before becoming his mistress, was a 'sly prostitute' (i.e. not a common prostitute). All of which leaves us, after much thought, floundering, as usual, in deep waters. But interesting. Sex usually is.

....
* Accessed June 2017.
† In *Victorians Undone* (2017).

AFTERTHOUGHT
'Tresses'

Having pondered Dracula's chameleon moustache (see page 18) one can spend some time on Mina and Lucy's tresses (a word never applied to a man, however long his locks). Lucy's tresses, before her violation, are described as 'sunny' – as golden as those of the unfallen Eve. After Dracula has done his deed of darkness her hair turns brown. When she rises from her tomb, to bite the innocent, fair-haired, children of Hampstead, her hair is as black as hell.

The colour codes speak for themselves. Yet the blonde vampire in Castle Dracula still provokes curiosity. Is she, so to speak, a virgin? Will her golden tresses darken after feasting on Jonathan? What colour is her hair when Van Helsing plunges his stake into her heart? Unanswered questions, alas.*

----

* I am obliged to Charlotte Hansen's blog post 'Hair Color and Innocence in Bram Stoker's Dracula', available online.

Is Dracula's blood warm?

꤀꤀

Is he, put another way, literally cold-blooded? In one of the most vivid scenes in the novel Jonathan, facing another disturbed night, looks out of the window of the castle and sees a head emerging from the window below him:

> my very feelings changed to repulsion and terror when I saw the whole man slowly emerge from the window and begin to crawl down the castle wall over that dreadful abyss, *face down*, with his cloak spreading out around him like great wings. At first I could not believe my eyes. I thought it was some trick of the moonlight, some weird effect of shadow; but I kept looking, and it could be no delusion. I saw the fingers and toes grasp the corners of the stones, worn clear of the mortar by the stress of years, and by thus using every projection and inequality move downwards with considerable speed, just as a lizard moves along a wall.
>
> What manner of man is this, or what manner of creature is it in the semblance of man?

Lizards need sunlight to generate their energy. If there is one thing Count Dracula does not need it is sunlight.

During the day, in London, he wears a panama (no film version has dared picture that sartorial detail). Dracula's face, all reports testify, is unnaturally pale – a hue associated with cold skin. He exudes, in manner, a corpse-like frigidity, except immediately after devouring when he resembles a fat filthy leech. Warm blood, cold blood? What runs through his veins? *Buffy the Vampire Slayer* and associated websites torment themselves with this blood puzzle incessantly. It makes a big difference in the love scenes and 'Yuk!' factor. The fact that, as Jonathan notes on their first meeting, the Count's hand is 'as cold as ice' provokes merely a minor shudder.

In the final scene, Quincey's bowie knife goes for the heart. Does Dracula have one? Or is the stolen blood in his body still and cooling fast. These anatomical speculations, which the novel does little to clarify, lead on to the larger question, does a vampire's blood circulate, as ours does?

Blood, after all, is what the vampiric kind live on. But does their own blood get pumped around the body to its extremities? Put another way, how, anatomically, does the undead corpus (corpse) handle its unlife-blood?

As I say, tormenting questions. Turn, for enlightenment, to the 'Federal Vampire and Zombie Agency', the bible of straight-faced speculation on such issues.* These are the authoritative answers to the above questions:

....
* https://www.fvza.org/science2.html

Blood:

Vampire blood is called ichor (pr. ik-er), and appears more brown or black due to an increase in iron and bile levels, allowing it to carry more oxygen and clot faster while slowing the growth of harmful microbes.

Heart:

Vampire blood is pumped via the contraction of skeletal muscle rather than the heart, which eventually atrophies from disuse. At rest, these contractions are mostly involuntary and take place in the limbs, emanating from the furthest extremities inward, like a wave. BPM for each contraction tends to be much lower than the average human heartbeat.

Adrenaline:

This 'emergency hormone', produced by the adrenal glands, is released in consistently large amounts in vampire blood during 'fight-or-flight' situations. This quickly raises a vampire's sluggish metabolism by increasing blood flow, dilating air passages and accelerating the production of clotting factors. Along with changes in muscle, bone and connective tissue, this ability to release adrenaline only adds to a vampire's extraordinary power.

Now we know.

Why are Dracula's
palms hirsute?

ᚬᚼᚼ

Harker gives us a number of eyewitness sketches of his
sinister host. It is not easy, since Dracula's appearance
is fluid as quicksilver and radically metamorphic. As Stoker
records in his surviving notes, it has proved impossible to
create a picture of the Count. The image dissolves on the
canvas.

One detail in his pseudo-human manifestations does, however, catch the eye as something fixed:

> Hitherto I [Jonathan] had noticed the backs of his
> hands as they lay on his knees in the firelight, and
> they had seemed rather white and fine; but seeing
> them now close to me, I could not but notice that
> they were rather coarse – broad, with squat fingers.
> Strange to say, there were hairs in the centre of the
> palm. The nails were long and fine, and cut to a sharp
> point. As the Count leaned over me and his hands
> touched me, I could not repress a shudder.

He is being fondled, he senses, by something inhuman.
Evolution has bred out in the human race the growth of hair

on the palm and soles of the feet, other than for a few unfortunates suffering from what is called Hypertrichosis.*

The primary explanation for Dracula having inhumanly hairy palms is that in his early thinking Bram Stoker was in two minds as to whether the Count should be a werewolf (lycanthrope), a vampire, or something in between. As a relic of this uncertainty Dracula has the telltale unibrow associated with the werewolf. 'His eyebrows', we are told, are 'very massive, almost meeting over the nose'.

Stoker picked up all the lore a novelist could need about werewolves from his friend, the scholar Sabine Baring-Gould. (Baring-Gould was an Exeter resident and it has been surmised that Stoker put Harker's office in the shadow of Exeter Cathedral as a tribute.) In his classic *Book of Werewolves* (1865) Baring-Gould describes the humanoid werewolf's palms exactly as Stoker describes Dracula's palms: 'the werewolf has broad hands, short fingers and has some hairs in the hollow of his hand.'

Like the devil's cloven foot, the inhumanly hairy paw witnesses to the werewolf within. Reach for your silver bullets, Quincey.

A clear fragment of this werewolf conception remains in the early lupine episode, as Dracula is driving Harker at breakneck speed to his castle. The moon breaks, glisteningly, through the clouds to shine as light as day; suddenly the coach is surrounded by a ring of wolves, slavering for human meat.

....
* Hyperthricosis has been given a relevant nickname: 'werewolf syndrome'.

The driver (it is Dracula, we shall later discover) leaves his seat to confront the beasts:

> How he came there, I know not, but I heard his voice raised in a tone of imperious command, and looking towards the sound, saw him stand in the roadway. As he swept his long arms, as though brushing aside some impalpable obstacle, the wolves fell back and back further still. Just then a heavy cloud passed across the face of the moon, so that we were again in darkness.

'Imperious'? He is clearly the alpha wolf, the *werewolf*. One notices that in this confrontation Dracula is at his most hirsute, with a heavy beard. Underneath his large hat he will certainly have the telltale unibrow.

Stoker did not, however, develop this concept in the narrative. When he lands in Whitby, Dracula is a large dog, possibly a small wolf; not ostensibly werewolfian. Stoker was, to put it simply, keeping two narrative balls in the air until the second half of the novel.

One reason the lupine theme did not, in the event, work for Stoker is because the emergence of the werewolf depends on long-separated lunar phases. Dracula is nocturnal – any night is vampire night. And Dracula can, as a vampire, change into more things than man's four-legged, hairy enemy. It makes for a more rapid narrative and interesting contest between the Count (Dracula) and the Professor (Van Helsing).

One of the things which constantly strikes one, on a thoughtful reading of the novel, is how Stoker, while writing, kept in play a range of different narrative possibilities. Dracula the hairy wolf-man is one he did not develop, nor fully erase. It was narrative ammunition not fired but always at the ready.

Dracula's hairy palms: a second reason

There is another aspect to Dracula's hairy palms. The sin of Onan. Early European society was obsessed with the vice – or was it a disease? – of self-abuse, to use the coyest phrase. (There are, of course, enough un-coy names to fill a small encyclopedia.)

A classic, and in its time hugely influential, warning was that proclaimed by the Swiss physician Samuel Tissot in his *L'Onanisme, ou Dissertation physique sur les maladies produites par la masturbation* (1754). Among the deadly '*maladies produites par la masturbation*' which parents and physicians should keep their eyes open for, given the incorrigible secretiveness of the self-abuser, were pallor and daytime debilitation verging, in its extreme, on paralysis. The Onanist reduces himself by his manual malpractice to 'a being that less resembled a living creature than a corpse ... it was difficult to discover that he had formerly been part of the human race'. If not un-dead then certifiably un-living. And the guilty hand of the chronic masturbator would be (hairily) marked – like Cain's forehead. A sign conspicuous of God's curse on the vile manual practice.

Fear of masturbation reached phobic heights in the 19th century. That the hairy palm was a giveaway was widespread lore (it survives to this day as a schoolboy joke). Since this hairiness was rarely actually seen, other than by those given to the solitary vice, as the shameless Rousseau called it, the afflicted would, presumably skim over their palms every day with their morning razor. Ladies might presumably epilate.

Britain and America – in fact all countries who had undergone a Puritan moral revolution – were obsessed about the horrible consequences of self-abuse. Machines were developed, more complex than the legendary female chastity belt, to keep the dreaded vice at bay (the 'Stephenson Spermatic Truss' was one such). The Kellogg brothers, fanatical on the subject to the point of lunacy, touted their corn flakes as a sovereign preservative.* Involuntary nocturnal emission, spermatorrhea, was usefully controlled by such machinery and dietary measures. Dracula evinces all the signs of a chronic self-abuser: pallor, night-walking, enfeeblement during daylight hours. And, of course, that giveaway hairy palm. Corn flakes would not, one fears, help.

One of the explanations for adult masturbation being epidemic in the male Victorian population was late marriage. Another was segregated education. Lucy's three suitors are all, we can safely assume, around thirty; she is not yet twenty. Are Arthur, Quincey and Jack to simply cross their legs? Or have recourse to ladies of easy virtue? Or simply make use of the ever-ready Mrs Hand? Look at their palms and see. Myself,

---

* A comic novel on the Kellogg brothers' mission to heal the private parts of America, *The Road to Wellville* by T.C. Boyle, was published in 1993.

I would conjecture the judicious and discreet use of expensive courtesans – at least by Arthur and Quincey; Jack Seward seems cut from different, more moralistic, cloth.

The most thorough exploration of this topic, historically, with illuminating sidelights on to *Dracula* is Deborah Mary Birch's jaunty article 'Hairy Palms, or, Onania and all its Frightful Consequences' (which I am gratefully plundering).*

Birch notes, as I hadn't, that in later versions and all the leading screen versions the hairy palm detail is removed. It could, some editor may have realised, inspire sniggers rather than shudders. But one should recall that in May 1897 it was still a shuddery subject.

Hair has the unique feature of being both inside and outside the body. And it surrounds human genitalia. The evolutionary reason for this is not clear. Eyebrows (to keep sweat out of eyes while hunting) are, by contrast, quite explicable. We can surmise that the hairy palm suggests, vaguely but powerfully, as does pubic hair, sexuality. As do the werewolf's lunar 'monthlies'. As Birch notes:

> The sexual symbolism of both the wolfman and Dracula is hard to miss; monthly attacks that can be measured by the cycle of the moon, sexual and (when appropriate) homoerotic connotations of blood sucking – the red substance often compared to that invaluable life source, semen. In an attempt to

* http://www.academia.edu/6291687/Hairy_Palms_or_Onania_and_all_its_Frightful_Consequences.

hide their true nature, werewolves often shaved their palm but hair, insubordinate foe, grows back; *watch for stubbled hands*, we are warned. [Birch's italics]

And warned we shall be.

Is Dracula gay?

T he question has, of course, been asked over and again. Two factors are relevant in attempting any answer. Most noteworthy is that Stoker worked all his professional life in a world – that of the London theatre – which was uniquely tolerant of homosexuality. There has been much speculation as to the relationship of Henry Irving and Stoker, his acolyte and personal servant. And what else? Stoker probably saw the actor naked, in the dressing room, more often than he did his wife in the bedroom.

Stoker might have adventured down this path – the love that dare not write its three-volume novel – to do something genuinely groundbreaking. He did not. It is more than likely that he was inhibited by a historical event, and his personal connection with it.

The 1890s saw the downfall of Stoker's friend, and one-time love rival from Dublin days, Oscar Wilde. Wilde's action for libel against the Marquis of Queensberry for labelling him a 'somdomite' was opened on 3 April 1895. It ended in loss for Wilde. The second, vengeful trial, brought against Wilde by the state for gross indecency, took place three weeks later. It inspired speeches by the defendant from the witness box, gallantly defending the freedom to love where love took a man.

The jury could not decide. It led to a third trial, which opened on 22 May 1895 and a less enlightened twelve jurors (all men; statistically there would have been a gay among them). Wilde was found guilty and sentenced to two years' hard labour.

He was released on 19 May 1897, three weeks before Stoker's novel was released. The Wilde trials inspired a manic horror at sodomy across the nation – a moral panic, no less. Wilde and his 'vice' had no public defenders the length and breadth of the land in August 1897. Nor was there sympathy for works of literature such as *The Picture of Dorian Gray*, which were wholly lax on 'the unspeakable crime of the Oscar Wilde sort', as the hero calls it in E.M. Forster's *Maurice* (a book he could not publish in the Edwardian period in which he was writing it without fear of prosecution).

For Stoker it was a tricky problem. By 1897, when Dracula was published, he had had two years to work out what precautions a wise author would take. He and Wilde were known to be friends. Many knew that the two of them had been suitors for the same woman, Florence Balcombe, now Stoker's wife. He obliterated from the novel any possible tincture of gay.

But perhaps not entirely. Discussion about Dracula being gay or not has centred on one particular clue the novel seems to throw the reader's way. When he comes down to rein in his concubines, slavering as they are to ravish Jonathan, there is an angry exchange between the vampiric sultan and his harem. 'You yourself never loved; you never love!' angrily protests one:

On this the other women joined, and such a mirth-less, hard, soulless laughter rang through the room that it almost made me [Jonathan, recalling the event in his diary] faint to hear; it seemed like the pleasure of fiends. Then the Count turned, after looking at my face attentively, and said in a soft whisper:–

'Yes, I too can love; you yourselves can tell it from the past. Is it not so? Well, now I promise you that when I am done with him you shall kiss him at your will. Now go! go! I must awaken him, for there is work to be done.'

Clearly Dracula has a taste for Jonathan Harker's blood. When he sees his guest with a shaving cut, as Jonathan relates, 'his eyes blazed with a sort of demoniac fury, and he suddenly made a grab at my throat'. But he leaves the vulnerable Englishman's neck unbitten all the weeks Jonathan is resident in his castle. Nothing would be easier than to drop a 'potion' in his guest's nightcap and, when the legal business is signed and sealed, suck him dry as a bone.

And that 'soft whisper' surely hints at something erotic stirring within. But Dracula never takes advantage of his help-less victim. Nor of any male: not even poor Renfield, who is desperate for his master's jugular kiss and the 'perpetual life' that comes with it.

There are possible explanations. One is that Dracula does not want Jonathan to be mentally disabled before the legal business is all dealt with. A terminally anaemic solicitor's clerk might be below his best on the finer points of property law. Another, as argued elsewhere (see page 130), is that Dracula needs Jonathan as a model Englishman to style himself on. That is all he wants to suck out of him.

Most probable, at the authorial level, is that Stoker simply did not dare take the risk of tarring himself with Wildeism.

An 'unspeakable vice of the Oscar Wilde kind', did Forster call it? So be it. Stoker would not speak of it in his novel. Nonetheless he would intrude, *sotto voce*, the merest hint for the smart reader. That 'soft whisper' echoes suggestively in the reader's mind.

What is 'Carfax'?

ᘏᓭᘏ

O xonians will have no problem in firing off the answer. It is the crossroads at the centre of their city, a spot redolent with history – some of it as cruel (the public burning of the 'heretics' Latimer and Ridley, for example, in front of a jeering crowd) as anything Vlad Tepes could come up with.

The word 'carfax' is not, generally, used to describe locations elsewhere than at the heart of Oxford. Etymologically the word can be traced to the French *quatre faces*, four faces. It's a very high-table name. Dracula, we may note in passing, has four visages at least, changing with whatever situation he finds himself in.

Jonathan is confronted with the first of those faces when his host, masquerading as an excessively hairy coachman, picks him up at a crossroads – the Borgo Pass. It symbolises. One road leads to safety; the other to damnation. Jonathan makes the wrong choice. A forced move, as they say in chess. Dracula has already tossed his luggage on to the coach.

The Castle Dracula Hotel now proudly claims to be located on that very pass: a sinister hostelry, one might think, to rank with the Overlook Hotel in Stephen King's *The Shining*. Some TripAdvisor reviewers (particularly the one cited prominently, who complained about the staff being 'ignorant') are doubtless frozen into photographs on the Hotel Castle Dracula walls, like King's Jack Torrance, one can fantasise.*

On his wild ride to Castle Dracula Jonathan passes a number of cross-shrines. His English, Protestant eye will find them offensive. They are routinely located at crossroads, symbolising roads taken/not taken in life. Both vampires and werewolves (the Count, at this stage is ambiguously both) are, lore has it, magnetically drawn to carfaxes/crossroads. As the authoritative website Werewolves.com informs us:

> Many of the lobisomem [the Brazilian word for werewolves, if you did not know it] legends have to do with how one transforms into a beast, and then transforms back. In many of these legends, the lobisomem will turn when they get to a crossroads on Friday night at midnight, full moon or no. In order to get back into man form, the lobisomem must find the same crossroads where they originally turned into the savage beast. And still, in other areas of the country, it's believed that a lobisomem must run through seven cemeteries before they can be transformed back.

Vampires share a traditional interest in crossroads. As does the Devil, of course. Robert Johnson, the greatest blues singer in history, allegedly sold his soul at a Delta crossroads, in return

---

* King's novel echoes throughout with elements from *Dracula* as does his early Vampire novel, *Salem's Lot* (1975). King recalled beginning to write it after teaching *Dracula* to a high school class.

for his mastery over the 'Devil's Music'. The authoritative website Vampires.com (we're lucky to be living in this internet age) tells us all we need to know. And more:

> For ages crossroads have been considered places for evil activity. A known meeting place for the unholy. Crossroads are unhallowed ground haunted by demons, the Devil, witches, fairies, ghosts, spirits, and of course, vampires. In Russian folklore, the undead were believed to wait at crossroads, drinking the blood of weary travelers unlucky enough [to] pass their way. In Romanian lore, living vampires, those who are destined to become vampires after death, send their souls out of their bodies at night to wander crossroads.

Supposed vampires were routinely, like suicides, buried at crossroads and staked fast to the dirt – because 'it was believed that once they rose, they wouldn't know which path to take back home'. Dracula is not, of course, a stupid vampire. If he doesn't know where to go he studies his Bradshaw.

Dracula chooses to reside in Carfax from the available properties his estate agent has shown him. The old ruin has everything a vampire could want: pre-eminently, sacred earth round its decayed chapel, and the 'quatre faces'. Dracula can never have too many cruxes, it would seem. On his way to Carfax he travels via King's Cross, Charing Cross, and stays for a few recuperative days in a new refrigerated storage warehouse at Cross Angel Street. He likes cold. And cross-streets.

There is, of course, a paradox in Dracula's relationship with the cross which I have been unable to make sense of. The cross is a potent vampire repellent. The innkeeper's wife gives Jonathan a crucifix. Out of politeness he (wisely) takes and wears it, despite an Anglican twinge of conscience. He later writes in his journal:

> Bless that good, good woman who hung the crucifix round my neck! For it is a comfort and a strength to me whenever I touch it. It is odd that a thing which I have been taught to regard with disfavour and as idol-atrous should in a time of loneliness and trouble be of help. Is it that there is something in the essence of the thing itself, or that it is a medium, a tangible help, in conveying memories of sympathy and comfort? Some time, if it may be, I must examine this matter and try to make up my mind about it.*

For Van Helsing (a cradle Catholic) the crucifix is as potent a weapon against Dracula as his trusty hammer and wooden stake. As I say, the contradiction teases. Does Dracula love or hate the cross? I would be grateful for answers.

....
* Commentators note Francis Ford Coppola's elaborate play with Catholic symbolism – particularly the cross – in his take on *Dracula* and assume, as with *The Godfather*, he is exploring his own religious upbringing. In passages like the above Jonathan seems on the point of converting.

Where would you find a 'gesunder' in *Dracula*?

≈≈≈

Virtually every Victorian bedroom had them. Outside lavatories, and the absence of night-lights, made them necessary.

'Gesunders', they were called: the thing that 'goes under' the bed. Even, unromantically, on the couple's honeymoon. I can remember the ones in my grandparents' house being emptied of a morning, a napkin decently covering the contents. I worked, one 1950s summer, in a seaside Clacton hotel. I remember an old housemaid weeping because she had been told that she must empty chamber pots containing 'number twos', or be sacked.

Chamber pots, not trousers, were the true Victorian unmentionables. And yet, strangely, they are mentioned in *Dracula*. In Stoker's surviving notes there is a huge amount of material about Whitby along with page after page of Yorkshire dialect words and their meanings, which clearly fascinated him.

There are many bedroom scenes in Dracula. But it is not in one of those that our gesunder is briefly glimpsed. Mina and a local Whitby resident – an old man almost as garrulous as Van Helsing – have the following exchange in a churchyard.

Mr Swales has lived long enough to have a wholly cynical view of the human condition; particularly in Whitby.

> 'Yabblins! There may be a poorish few not wrong, savin' where they make out the people too good; for there be folk that do think a balm-bowl be like the sea, if only it be their own. The whole thing be only lies. Now look you here; you come here a stranger, an' you see this kirk-garth.' I nodded, for I thought it better to assent, though I did not quite understand his dialect. I knew it had something to do with the church. He went on: 'And you consate that all these steans be aboon folk that be happed here, snod an' snog?' I assented again. 'Then that be just where the lie comes in. Why, there be scores of these lay-beds that be toom as old Dun's 'bacca-box on Friday night.' He nudged one of his companions, and they all laughed.

The churchyard, Swales means, has many empty coffins. Largely because Whitby sailors die at sea and their human remains have been committed to the waves. But their families must have something to grieve over. Hence the empty coffins and (as Swales sees it) needless funerary expense.

The inhabited or uninhabited grave is thematically central in *Dracula*. But what is a 'balm-bowl'? Translated from Whitbyese it means chamber pot – literally, 'ease bowl'.

Stoker must have chortled as he slipped the naughtiness in, as discreetly as the object itself under the Victorian bed.

Why is Dracula so interested in blue flames?

⋙⋘

The novel opens with Jonathan Harker describing in his morning diary the biggest event in his life. His trip to Transylvania will, in the event, prove an even bigger event than the young man anticipates.

He arrives, fresh from a first-class train experience through strange landscapes (his client, Dracula, stints nothing in expenses, we may assume), a goggle-eyed tourist, a freshly bought Baedecker guide in hand, on his way to Transylvania.* The Carpathians loom. Sinister. No trains run there.

He packs away a good meal at the Golden Krone Hotel in Bistritz, leaving the next day on St George's Eve. The date is a pleasant coincidence for a red-blooded Englishman. Mythologically the Transylvanian St George does what he does in all countries where he is celebrated. The saint in armour rescues an imprisoned maiden (representing civilisation) from a dragon's cave (representing barbarism). And what does the word 'Dracul' mean in Romanian? Dragon. And 'Dracula'? Son of Dragon. Thought-provoking.

....

* The text reveals that Stoker used Baedecker for scene setting, often transcribing from the guide verbatim.

St George is otherwise known as 'Red Crosse', rendered famous in the first book of Spenser's *The Fairy Queene*. There is something of the Red Crosse Knight about Jonathan Harker. It goes along with a running Manichean subplot in *Dracula*, God versus the Devil, outcome, as ever, uncertain.

On the last leg of Jonathan's journey, now deep in the heart of Skezely tribal territory, darkness is falling on St George's Eve. Like the related German/Austrian Walpurgisnacht, it is a 'Witches' Sabbath'. Traditionally all hell is let loose on these nights.*

A mysterious driver (Dracula himself, we later learn) picks up an increasingly jittery Harker at a crossroads: a 'carfax'. The coach drives round and round, going nowhere, until the stroke of midnight. Ominous hour. Dogs howl, wolves prowl, bats swarm, Harker shivers. Snow falls – in May? The driver leaves his vehicle to confront a bloodthirsty pack of wolves. They are obedient to the driver's red-eyed glare, snuffing the dominant werewolf, and slink off. They know an alpha when they see one.

The bushy-bearded driver returns to his seat and his by now wholly petrified passenger, thinking desperately about return tickets to St Pancras station. It is too late. Then the *calèche* in which he is being driven stops yet again. Will this journey never end? The driver, it seems, wants to investigate something mysterious, which he has glimpsed. As a bamboozled Harker records in his next morning's diary:

....

* See http://www.jasoncolavito.com/transylvanian-superstitions.html.

Suddenly, away on our left, I saw a faint flickering blue flame. The driver saw it at the same moment; he at once checked the horses, and, jumping to the ground, disappeared into the darkness. I did not know what to do, the less as the howling of the wolves grew closer; but while I wondered the driver suddenly appeared again, and without a word took his seat, and we resumed our journey. I think I must have fallen asleep and kept dreaming of the incident, for it seemed to be repeated endlessly, and now looking back, it is like a sort of awful nightmare. Once the flame appeared so near the road, that even in the darkness around us I could watch the driver's motions. He went rapidly to where the blue flame arose – it must have been very faint, for it did not seem to illumine the place around it at all – and gathering a few stones, formed them into some device. Once there appeared a strange optical effect: when he stood between me and the flame he did not obstruct it, for I could see its ghostly flicker all the same. This startled me, but as the effect was only momentary, I took it that my eyes deceived me straining through the darkness.

Why has the soil of Transylvania turned itself into a gigantic gas-fired hob? Stoker picked this lore-detail up, and made a powerful scene out of it, again from 'Madame Dracula', Emily Gerard. More specifically from her article 'Transylvanian Superstitions' in *The Nineteenth Century* magazine (1885) and her follow-up travel book, *The Land Beyond the Forest: Facts, Figures, and Fancies from Transylvania* (1888). She, unlike the author of *Dracula*, had lived in Dracula's country. Stoker lifted plentifully from her first-hand accounts without acknowledgement (all's fair in love and horror fiction).

As Dracula explains later to Harker, the soil of the region is blood-soaked and wars have left many residues of lost treasure. Emily Gerard fills out the accompanying 'x marks the spot' scenario with rich detail:

> In the night of St. George's Day (so say the legends) all these treasures begin to burn, or, to speak in mystic language, to 'bloom' in the bosom of the earth, and the light they give forth, described as a bluish flame resembling the colour of lighted spirits of wine, serves to guide favoured mortals to their place of concealment. The conditions to the successful raising of such a treasure are manifold, and difficult of accomplishment. In the first place, it is by no means easy for a common mortal who has not been born on a Sunday nor at midday when the bells are ringing, to hit upon a treasure at all. If he does, however, catch sight of a flame such as I have described, he must quickly stick a knife through the swaddling rags of his right foot, and then throw the knife in the direction of the flame he has seen. If two people are together during this discovery they must not on any account break silence till the treasure is removed, neither is it allowed to fill

up the hole from which anything has been taken, for that would induce a speedy death.

Dracula is no 'common mortal'. He can follow the flames without having to stab his right foot or any of the folderol Gerard describes. We may suspect he has gone blue-flame hunting many times before on the nights they blaze.

There are a couple of puzzles that remain: (1) Why has Dracula not arranged for his gypsy hirelings to bring Harker to the castle? (2) Why has Dracula arranged it that Harker arrives on this particular night, 4 May?

The simplest reason might be that Jonathan – or, rather, his coach driver from Bistritz – has jumped the gun. The first words Dracula says are 'You are early to-night, my friend'. From which we may deduce that Dracula originally intended to get to work with his shovel on the outward journey, picking up Jonathan when dawn breaks.*

There are other explanations. One of them is that Stoker, a man of the theatre to the core, wanted *son et lumière*: the wolves howl – sweet music, Dracula calls it – and flames light the way to the ruined castle. Bluntly, it is an 'effect' to amaze and tantalise the reader. Which it does.

The second reason, banally, is that Dracula is currently strapped for cash. He is embarking on a big adventure. It will not be a cheap adventure. The Count has, Harker discovers in his illicit tours round the castle, a secret treasure room.

....

* Dracula has normal human abilities in daytime, if he intends to use them. Early morning would be a more likely time for the coach to depart.

> The only thing I found was a great heap of gold in one corner – gold of all kinds, Roman, and British, and Austrian, and Hungarian, and Greek and Turkish money, covered with a film of dust, as though it had lain long in the ground. None of it that I noticed was less than three hundred years old. There were also chains and ornaments, some jewelled, but all of them old and stained.

An impressive heap. But one does rather wonder how Count Dracula is going to convert this museum-worthy wealth into the ready money required to buy a property in England in 1893. The Roman denarius had not, for 1,500 years, been coin of the realm.

Dracula is in the process of buying a large estate in England – 'Carfax' – and many other expensive pieces of real estate in the capital. He is leasing an entire schooner, the good ship (Dracula will make it something else) *Demeter*, for transporting his 50 boxes of Transylvanian dirt to England.

His ultimate aim? To conquer England; to do to it what Attila would have done. Make it part of Imperium Dracula. He and his paladins will suck humanity dry. World conquest will, in the long run, involve millions. Every little helps: hence Dracula's interest, on the night of 4 May 1893, in mysterious incandescence in the Transylvanian wilderness. Money, always money.

How does Vampire Lucy escape from a lead-lined coffin?

๛

If Stoker made a list of his favourite writers the name at the top, it is fair to guess, would be Edgar Allan Poe. *Dracula* manifestly owes greatly to Poe's 'Ligeia', for example. Poe's fable tells the story of a vampire wife who will not lie still in her vault (under the ruined mansion) but comes back to possess the person of her successor in the marital bed.

'Ligeia' is written with an eeriness of effect Stoker would have been the first to admire. The story went on to inspire (if that's right word) the finest of Roger Corman's schlock-horror films, starring the master of sinister, Vincent Price.*

Like Poe, Stoker was fascinated by the coffin as a fetish object. That final destination wooden box fascinates and is feared. As mentioned previously (see page 110), the fear of being buried while still alive was widespread in the 19th century. It led to ingeniously engineered coffins with bells, message pulls, and air-holes. The horror of undead interment is immortalised in one of the simplest and most powerful of Poe's tales: 'The Premature Burial'.

....

* The 1982 film *The Tomb of Ligeia* is available on YouTube and well worth visiting.

One of the myths about vampire extermination Stoker did not pursue was that they can be killed by shooting a firearm into their coffin. With his maxim gun, Quincey could reduce any off-the-shelf 19th-century coffin to matchwood. But perhaps not with a mere six-shooter. And if we're talking Lucy Westenra's coffin, almost certainly not.

In *Dracula* the undead Lucy – 'the bloofer lady' as her brood of Hampstead kids call her – does not roam nightly from an interred coffin, under two tons of soil. It would be something of a challenge for her to get out of a night, unless she metamorphosed into a mole.

Lucy has been laid in the Westenra family vault, on an elevated, waist-high, plinth. The description her unrestful resting place is quite precise. This is how it is described by Seward (forgive a lengthy quotation):

> At last we reached the wall of the churchyard, which we climbed over. With some little difficulty – for it was very dark, and the whole place seemed so strange to us – we found the Westenra tomb. The Professor took the key, opened the creaky door, and standing back, politely, but quite unconsciously, motioned me to precede him. There was a delicious irony in the offer, in the courtliness of giving preference on such a ghastly occasion. My companion followed me quickly, and cautiously drew the door to, after carefully ascertaining that the lock was a falling, and not a spring, one. In the latter case we should have been in a bad plight.

Then he fumbled in his bag, and taking out a matchbox and a piece of candle, proceeded to make a light. The tomb in the day-time, and when wreathed with fresh flowers, had looked grim and gruesome enough; but now, some days afterwards, when the flowers hung lank and dead, their whites turning to rust and their greens to browns; when the spider and the beetle had resumed their accustomed dominance; when time-discoloured stone, and dust-encrusted mortar, and rusty, dank iron, and tarnished brass, and clouded silver-plating gave back the feeble glimmer of a candle, the effect was more miserable and sordid than could have been imagined. It conveyed irresistibly the idea that life – animal life – was not the only thing which could pass away.

Van Helsing went about his work systematically. Holding his candle so that he could read the coffin plates, and so holding it that the sperm dropped in white patches which congealed as they touched the metal, he made assurance of Lucy's coffin. Another search in his bag, and he took out a turnscrew.

'What are you going to do?' I asked.

'To open the coffin. You shall yet be convinced.' Straightway he began taking out the screws, and finally lifted off the lid, showing the casing of lead beneath. The sight was almost too much for me. It seemed to be as much an affront to the dead as it would have been to have stripped off her clothing in her sleep whilst living; I actually took hold of his hand to stop him. He only said: 'You shall see,' and again fumbling in his bag, took out a tiny fret-saw. Striking the turnscrew through the lead with a swift downward stab, which made me wince, he made a small hole, which was, however, big enough to admit the point of the saw. I had expected a rush of gas from the week-old corpse. We doctors, who have had to study our dangers, have to become accustomed to such things, and I drew back towards the door. But the Professor never stopped for a moment; he sawed down a couple of feet along one side of the lead coffin, and then across, and down the other side. Taking the edge of the loose flange, he bent it back towards the foot of the coffin, and holding up the candle into the aperture, motioned to me to look.

I drew near and looked. The coffin was empty.

It is a grisly scene. The 'sperm' dripping on to the coffin jolts (Stoker could have used the unjolting word 'wax'). The scene also illumines the ways in which Victorians treated their dead – something that not all of us know nowadays. By law at the time, the coffins of those in vaults, above-ground tombs, or catacombs, tunnels beneath the earth, were required to be double or triple shelled (not counting the interior velvet padding). The inner, or middle, lining was sealed lead, as referred to by Seward in the above passage. Such a coffin could easily weigh a quarter of a ton.

The funereal flowers wilt in days. The wooden casing will be rotted in a few years. The lead is eternal. The body within will be well placed to emerge on solid ground and be first in line when the trumpets blow at the four corners of the earth for Judgement Day. 'Resurgam' was a popular inscription on Victorian tombstones. Lucy Westenra can conveniently 'resurge' every night of the week. But how does she get out of the lead shell? Is there some small aperture (a breathing hole?) in the metal for her to emerge in a Draculean mist? Van Helsing cannot find any. Nor is the lead casing around Lucy visibly damaged, until Van Helsing gets to work on it. Dracula himself can surely not drop by every night with a 'turnscrew' to release his newest apprentice. And once out there are problems for Lucy the Vampire. The door of the tomb, we are told, has a simple lift-lock on the inside. No problem getting out. Getting back in, at daybreak, though will be tricky, without a key. It is, one finally concludes, best not to concern oneself overly with such trivial details. Move on to important things.

But something lingers. Once read it is hard to forget this scene. Anything to do with coffins – that final box in which we exit the world – haunts the mind, as does the womb, the warm organ by which we entered. One can end, as this chapter began, with Poe's thrilling depiction of premature burial: the following, for example, testified to by a grisly disinterment in Baltimore:

> The lady was deposited in her family vault, which, for three subsequent years, was undisturbed. At the

expiration of this term it was opened for the reception of a sarcophagus; – but, alas! how fearful a shock awaited the husband, who, personally, threw open the door! As its portals swung outwardly back, some white-apparelled object fell rattling within his arms. It was the skeleton of his wife in her yet unmouldered shroud.

A careful investigation rendered it evident that she had revived within two days after her entombment; that her struggles within the coffin had caused it to fall from a ledge, or shelf to the floor, where it was so broken as to permit her escape. A lamp which had been accidentally left, full of oil, within the tomb, was found empty; it might have been exhausted, however, by evaporation. On the uttermost of the steps which led down into the dread chamber was a large fragment of the coffin, with which, it seemed, that she had endeavored to arrest attention by striking the iron door. While thus occupied, she probably swooned, or possibly died, through sheer terror; and, in falling, her shroud became entangled in some iron-work which projected interiorly. Thus she remained, and thus she rotted, erect.

The last four words chill like verbal ice. Stoker clearly knew his Poe backward, and echoes it in the depiction of Lucy's restless interment and final, decapitated and eviscerated rest. Resurgam in pieces.

Where have all the vampires gone?

⚬⚬⚬

They are rare birds. If, as Van Helsing says, one bite and you're 'turned', and go on to be a biter yourself, there ought to be more vampires in Transylvania than starlings. Exponential, my dear Watson. But one of the oddities of the Romanian vampire community is that they simply aren't there. We meet just four long-toothed Transylvanian locals in the novel: the Count and the weird sisters. This after 600 years ravaging?

On the good ship (bad ship it turns out) *Demeter* Dracula destroys 50 or so mariners. None of them seem to become vampires. Just corpses. Whitby's dogs are at risk for a while: but the local community is apparently unscathed from the enemy of mankind roaming free among them. In London Dracula's score (two ladies and, via one of them, some Hampstead urchins) is minimal, given the 1890s level of metropolitan crime. Jack the Ripper outdoes Dracula three to one. How, one wonders, is the Count keeping body and soul (if he has one) together during his London sojourn?

To ask a simple question why haven't vampires, given the millennia at their disposal, taken over the whole human show?

I have, as it happens, pondered this question before (in my 1999 book *Who Betrays Elizabeth Bennet?*). Then, in the absence of any entirely satisfying answer, I put forward some speculative suggestions including the following:

It is clear, in the last stages of the action, that Mina is a very special kind of victim. As a mark (literally) of her singularity, she has taken part in a gruesome blood-exchange ceremony with the count ... It seems that, by taking back the blood which he earlier took from her, she has become one of a privileged caste of living victims – one who seems to have some of the powers of the Un-Dead while still alive. Mina manifestly has super-human powers – a radar-like apprehension of where Dracula is, for example. She is 'unclean' – the Christian cross burns her skin like acid. Her teeth have become sharper, and she looks – from some angles – vampiric.

There is, one deduces, an inner élite of 'super vampires' who circulate Dracula's sacramental blood among themselves – true communicants in the horrible sect, and Mina is now one of them. It is only this small coterie which is immortal, we may speculate. The bulk of their victims are disposable nourishment – a kind of human blood-bank to be discarded when exhausted. Unfortunately, Stoker does not give us any clear warrant for this speculation, nor does he (as far as I can see) work it plausibly into his narrative.

Since then, I am pleased to report, the puzzle seems to have been exercising other minds (prompted, it would seem, by a more recent wave of vampire stories, none of which deals with the issue any more satisfactorily than did Stoker). In frivolous answer to the conundrum the following *jeu d'esprit* appeared in the normally unfrivolous *New Scientist*, under the headline 'Why Vampires Would Have a Population Problem':*

> Colleagues in the *New Scientist* office suggest that there must be a high death rate caused by Slayers and other natural hazards, balancing out the high 'birth' rate or mortals converted by bites. Such a mechanism could be modelled using the classic Lotka-Volterra equations for predator-prey populations. Although, of course, vampires are capable of making prey out of their supposed predators.
>
> However, I think a more plausible explanation is the tendency for vampires to involve themselves in doomed love affairs with slightly dotty young women, causing them to spend centuries mooning around in crypts not getting much done. An extreme case of this was recently documented in a dumb emo teen movie.
>
> This would mean that new vampires were only produced at a very low rate, allowing the population to remain fairly stable.

The Lotka-Volterra (I've checked, it's real) equation explains the balances, and mutually supportive survival achieved in

....
* The article, dated March 2009, is credited to Michael Marshall.

natural habitats between prey/predator species very elegantly. At least I think that is what it does. I can't understand it, even as laid out by Wikipedia, one's first point of call in such crises. Lotka-Volterra connects, we learn there, with the 'Kolmogorov model, which is a more general framework [modelling] the dynamics of ecological systems with predator–prey interactions, competition, disease, and mutualism'.*

It is, one concludes, very strange where an interest in *Dracula* ends you up in. Transylvania, Lotka-Volterra, the Kolmogorov model. At times this is not a novel for the simple-minded.

---

* Accessed June 2017.

Coincidence, or something else?

༄༅

Does Dracula (fore)know that Carfax is within a short bat's-flight from Dr Seward's asylum, and his straitjacketed slave, Renfield? Or is it merely coincidence?

Coincidence is common enough in Victorian literature. Many of its narratives could not run smoothly without it. The prime thinker about the phenomenon is Thomas Hardy, in his prose and poetry. In his best-known poem Britain constructs the world's greatest sea-liner, the *Titanic*. Simultaneously, Nature builds an iceberg. How does it happen these two objects will meet? Coincidence? Or destiny?

Hardy theorised the ubiquity of coincidence in human existence, and the world around us, as 'immanent will' – as outlined by his favourite philosopher, the arch-pessimist, Arthur Schopenhauer. The things around us have ingrained within them a drive, invisible to us, but destructive, mischievous or just downright contrary. They are programmed so that things turn out as they do. Coincidence is the proof of that.

There is in Hardy's universe no 'transcendant' entity (God, the Devil, or a crew of gods who play with us for their sport). That is mere myth. Most of us wrestle with what looks like immanence in our everyday lives. Things seem to have 'a will of their own'. Think of Laurel and Hardy, struggling to get the piano down a flight of stairs. The piano has no intention of letting them do it. Bloody instrument. Or Basil Fawlty, for whom the world is an assemblage of things designed by some malign force to frustrate Basil Fawlty.

I myself have a briefcase which maliciously hides things from me. (I can't get rid of it – it's a Tumi.) My crockery has an ingrained desire to hurl itself to the floor. And so on.

Stoker, unlike Hardy, does not subscribe to the immanence view. He is a transcendentalist. In Stoker's view of life, as expressed in *Dracula*, Satan and God are locked in a struggle to establish who is in charge. The world is their stake.* There is no question as to whose side the Count – a prize pupil in Satan's Scholasticon – is on. He is Team Devil to the roots of his teeth. There is all to play for. It is a Manichaean struggle (to continue with the big words) with transcendent players and the final outcome uncertain. This is Stoker's cosmogony.

There is nothing merely coincidental about the conjunction of events in *Dracula* – Mina, Lucy, and the Count all coming together in the remote town of Whitby, for example. Dracula somehow foreknew the ladies would be there. It's his design, Satan's design.

---

* In the Old Testament God and Satan embark on a wager, as to whether Job will sustain his belief, or succumb, after Satan does his worst. Neither supreme power knows what the outcome will be, apparently, any more than a gambler throwing dice.

In his notes Stoker inscribed the following aphorism from Sir Thomas Browne's *Religio Medici*: 'Many secrets there are in Nature of difficult discovery unto man, of easie knowledge unto Satan.' Dracula has manifest access to this 'easie knowledge'. It helps him; but it does not ensure victory.

How ordinary a vampire
is Count Dracula?

∽≪∾

In many ways, Count Dracula is a fairly run-of-the-mill vampire. He is humanoid, and can pass for one of us, even though, as Stoker's notes record, he only weighs, intrinsically, a couple of ounces, imperial.

He is, however, in one salient feature extraordinary. As Paul Barber reminds us, most European vampires were peasants and looked like peasants. They were often confused about what had happened to them. They were associated with infectious disease more often than exsanguination. Dracula is, whatever else you hold against him, classy. He could be your guest at the Athenaeum and not raise a patrician eyebrow.

There have been many exotic variations in the vampire kind as memorialised in folklore and elaborated in horror and fantasy fiction. Some are too exotic for everyone's taste. In the preface to his genre-bending sci-fi anthology *Dangerous Visions* (1967), Harlan Ellison, for example, recalls rejecting, with a shudder, a submitted story about a snot vampire. One's glad he did.

As Paul Barber reminds us, wherever human beings have formed societies they have imagined vampire co-habitants. But what human imagination has come up with is astonishingly diverse: a veritable *Wunderkammer* of vampiric oddity. Clive Leatherdale muses merrily on the theme:*

> In Asia, Chinese tales spoke of blood-sucking crea-
> tures that were green, covered with mould, and had
> a propensity to glow in the dark ... [In India,] The
> hant-pare would cling leech-like to the open wound
> of an injured person; while the vetala resembled an
> old hag and would seek the blood of sleeping women
> – for some reason preferring them drunk or insane.

Malaysia has an interesting variant:

> As the only apparatus indispensable to a vampire is a
> mouth and a stomach, the penangallen consisted of just
> a head, stomach, and dangling entrails. It would soar
> through the air to pursue its preferred victims: babies or
> women in labour ... Brazilians refer to a jaracara which
> resembles a snake and enjoys a penchant for either the
> blood or the milk of breast feeding mothers.

There is 'Bulgarian [talk] of a creature having just one nostril, a boneless frame, and fungoid flesh'. Leatherdale's jocularity is infectious. And by comparison with this menagerie Dracula strikes one as dull as ditchwater. A foreign count with teeth. Nothing special. Rather respectable, even.[†]

....

* In *Dracula: The Novel & the Legend* (1993).

[†] Those with any relish for more on this topic are directed to http://listverse.
com/2013/10/30/10-truly-creepy-vampires-from-around-the-world/

Is Van Helsing's giant spider real?

an Helsing is as much a tall-tale teller as a scientist. But just how tall are those tales? Consider the following. The Dutch sage is in conversation with Seward, lecturing as usual:

> Do you know all the mystery of life and death? Do you know the altogether of comparative anatomy and can say wherefore the qualities of brutes are in some men, and not in others? Can you tell me why, when other spiders die small and soon, that one great spider lived for centuries in the tower of the old Spanish church and grew and grew, till, on descending, he could drink the oil of all the church lamps?

The largest known spider, very rare, is *Theraphosa blondi*. It is known as the 'Goliath'. It is also nicknamed 'Bird-eater'. Its leg span can be a foot and its weight not far off half a pound. Rarely encountered by man, thank goodness, Goliath's habitat is the remoter regions of South America. It is nocturnal and lives in damp, dark places. Its skin is venomous to the touch and its two-inch fangs can penetrate and kill. And do. Its enormous size enables it to devour snakes and small birds.

It is eaten itself, as a delicacy, by locals; the flesh is described as 'shrimp-like'.

Dracula devotees, for whom no pebble is too small to look underneath, have tracked the source of Van Helsing's 'great spider' to the *Athenaeum* magazine, 1821, and the following wonder-of-the-day paragraph:

> The sexton of the church of St Eustace, at Paris, amazed to find frequently a particular lamp extinct early, and yet the oil consumed only, sat up several nights to discover the cause. At length he detected that a spider of surprising size came down the cord to drink the oil. A still more extraordinary instance of the same kind occurred during the year 1751, in the Cathedral of Milan. A vast spider was observed there, which fed on the oil of the lamps ... This spider, of four pounds weight, was sent to the Emperor of Austria, and placed in the Imperial Museum.

Stoker misremembers (the spider is located in France and Italy, not Spain). But how, one wonders, did he come across the reference in the first place? It is easier to think how, once read, it stuck in his mind. The 4lb spider (eight Goliaths in weight) symbolises, particularly in Van Helsing's erroneous version, the omnipresence of gluttonous Satan, even in the holiest places. The idea of this monster crawling out of crevices, down long ropes, in consecrated places to lap up holy oil, generates revulsion. The effect is deliberate, and tactical.

The perimeter of late Victorian disgust was something novelists had to be careful about. The Victorian gag reflex was more sensitive than ours. Indeed, there are several areas in Dracula where Stoker must have pondered how gross he dare make the text. Where did that red line lie? And where did Stoker feel it was safe to cross it? There is a relevant memo in the surviving notes:

(Mem leeches – attracted to Count D, and then repelled – develop idea)

He did not develop this 'mem' or refer to it again in his notes. The only reference to leeches in the novel is the description of Dracula lying in his coffin, after a feast of blood, 'like a filthy leech, exhausted with his repletion'.

How would Stoker have 'developed' the idea? The mental image of a leech-encrusted Dracula turns the stomach (mine, anyway).

To continue the revulsion theme, Renfield's diet is not good for the reader's gorge. He is a zoophagite. In a sense, so are most of us. Our mouths, as the Vegans righteously tell us, are the graves of living animals. Renfield's mouth is worse. A beefsteak, medium rare, is distantly related to what homo sapiens lived on in the hunter gatherer era. It makes us feel distant human origins. Renfield's diet identifies him as something less than human. In his notes Stoker calls him the 'fly-eater'. As he moves by gobbling his way up the evolutionary ladder he eats the spiders who have eaten his flies.

He is now on the arachnophage rung. He hopes to ascend, via birds which eat the insects, to a kitten which would eat the bird. Just like the little old lady in the nursery rhyme who swallowed a fly. Stoker may have toyed with the idea of Renfield as a felinophage, but pulled back at this point. He had reached the line. Crossing it would lead, by a few rungs, to cannibalism.

One can digress to note that Renfield was not alone in his eating preferences. The zoophagites, some of them eminent zoologists, were well known Victorian clubs devoted to feasting on exotic or otherwise interesting animals.

Occasionally there are catering experiments with insects. One can, for example, turn up web guides to the 'best bug restaurants' in New York. Grasshoppers modo mejicano, at The Black Ant, looks good. Renfield, however, eats his insects while still crawling, hopping and slithering. Uncooked. It is the life, not the calories he craves.

His lust for the life-giving fluid is displayed in the scene in which he cuts Seward's arm in a homicidal attack, and sups the spilled blood from the floor, before it loses its *elan vital*. He lifts his head, jaws dripping, to allude to scripture: 'the blood is the life,' he says.*

Renfield's transgressive appetite for blood is revealed only in this one, momentary, scene. Nonetheless, on the strength of it, Stoker's maniac has become the one of the few characters

---

* Deuteronomy 12, prohibiting the consumption of blood, 'for the blood is the life'.

in fiction who has donated his name to medicine.* There is a pleasantly owlish Wikipedia entry† on what is now called Renfield's syndrome which I can't resist quoting:

> Clinical vampirism, more commonly called Renfield's syndrome or Renfield syndrome, is an obsession with drinking blood. The earliest formal presentation of clinical vampirism to appear in the psychiatric literature, with the psychoanalytic interpretation of two cases, was contributed by Richard L. Vanden Bergh and John F. Kelley in 1964. As the authors point out, brief and sporadic reports of blood-drinking behaviors associated with sexual pleasure have appeared in the psychiatric literature at least since 1892 with the work of Austrian forensic psychiatrist Richard von Krafft-Ebing.

'At least since 1892' is an arresting detail. But it's not clear that Renfield, in 1897, suffers from Renfield's syndrome. He is wholly asexual and would be of no interest to Krafft-Ebing. His vampiric appetite for blood is only shown in the one scene with Seward's arm. Very disgusting it is but nonetheless a one-off thing.

---

* The only other I can think of is Pickwick Syndrome, named after the sleepy fat boy in Dickens's novel. It is more technically called Obesity Hypoventilation Syndrome.
† Accessed June 2017.

More typical of the man is Renfield's tidying up his cell for the arrival of Mina. Jack Seward is dictating to his trusty phonograph:

'She is going through the house, and wants to see every one in it,' I answered. 'Oh, very well,' he said; 'let her come in, by all means; but just wait a minute till I tidy up the place.' His method of tidying was peculiar: he simply swallowed all the flies and spiders in the boxes before I could stop him.

It's a darkly comic scene, if you can stomach it. Renfield obviously can.

Renfield is routinely seen as an acolyte – a holy idiot, whose existence is service to and adoration of his 'Lord and Master'. He has, one supposes, no more seen his Lord and Master than the average Christian has seen Christ in all his glory (yet). How Renfield has come by his reverential knowledge is a mystery.

Hilary Mantel's comments are obliquely enlightening on Renfield's saintly devotion:

Rudolph Bell's 1985 book *Holy Anorexia*, on Italian saints, is especially rewarding for connoisseurs of the spiritually lurid. St Maria Maddalena dei Pazzi lay naked on thorns. Catherine of Siena drank pus from a cancerous sore. One confessor ordered Veronica Giuliani to kneel while a novice of the order kicked her in the mouth. Another ordered her to clean the walls and floor of her cell with her tongue; but even he thought it was going too far when she swallowed the spiders and their webs.*

Which brings us back to where we began – to the *gobes mouches* (fly gobblers), as they are called in French. Spiders crawl everywhere in *Dracula*. They are recorded scuttling over Lucy's tomb: there are, if we dare think about it, flies feasting on her flesh within for them in turn to feast on.

Stoker pioneered, among much else, the uses to which fantasy literature could put the disgusting – in detail and conception. It is something to admire: with a momentary shudder. When one thinks about it, a furtively enjoyable shudder.

----

* https://www.theguardian.com/society/2004/mar/04/mentalhealth.health

Appendix:
Dracula Digested

by John Crace

John Crace is the parliamentary sketch writer for the Guardian
*newspaper, for which he also writes the regular Digested Read
feature. He is the author of several books including, with John
Sutherland, the multi-volume* The Incomplete Shakespeare.

Journal of Jonathan Harker

3 May–25 June: Wonderful meal in Buda-Pesth. (Note to
self: go back to restaurant to get recipe for Mina.) Then went
on to Transylvania to complete the property transaction for
Count Dracula. The maps weren't nearly as good as the British
Ordnance Survey ones so I was fearful I might be a little lost.
An old woman made the sign of the cross and started mut-
tering something about vampires. (Note to self: must ask the
Count about these superstitions.)

After venturing past brigands, wolves and blue flames, I
at last arrived at the castle where I was met by the Count. His
long, sharp, canine teeth were somewhat disconcerting. For
some reason I forgot to ask him about vampires. After a trou-
bled night's sleep I awoke to find that Dracula was nowhere to
be seen, so I made myself busy walking round the scary castle.

As a solicitor, I am being paid by the hour so it was no skin off my nose how long the job took; besides, I was also acting as an estate agent for the property so I wanted to make sure I got my 2 per cent of the final sale price.

Once the formalities were complete, I discovered to my horror that Count Dracula was crawling down a vertical wall in the manner of a lizard. Unless I was very much mistaken there was something sinister afoot. I tried to escape the castle, only to discover I was locked in. Only nearly escaped being attacked by three weird sisters who seemed rather sexually predatory. Then tried and failed to kill Dracula who was asleep in his coffin with fresh blood on his lips. Upset at being awoken, he left the castle with 50 boxes of dirt. Fell into a deep sleep.

Letter, Lucy Westenra to Mina Murray

24 May: Would you believe it? After not receiving a single offer of marriage in all my nineteen years, I today received three proposals on the same day from people who appeared to know each other better than I knew them. The first was from an American adventurer, Quincey Morris. I turned him down. The second was from Jack Seward, a doctor in charge of a lunatic asylum. I turned him down, too. The third was from Arthur Holmwood, heir to Lord Godalming. For some reason, I accepted this last offer. Can't think why.

Mina Murray's Journal

25 July–3 August: It has been so pleasant having Lucy and her mother to stay with me in Whitby, though I am most

concerned not to have heard from Jonathan since he left for Transylvania. Went down to the harbour where an old fisherman, Mr Swales, engaged me in conversation in a dialect I barely understood.

Dr Seward's Diary (kept in phonograph)

5 June: I am most concerned about one patient, R.M. Renfield, who suffers from zoophagy. He spends all his days consuming flies, spiders, sparrows and cats. I am still gutted Lucy turned me down.

Mina Murray's Journal

3–8 August: There has been a big storm that blew a Russian schooner, empty apart from her captain tied to the helm and quite dead, into the harbour. Some locals did say that a large dog was also seen leaping ashore. I am most perturbed by Lucy's behaviour, for at night she has taken to walking round Whitby in her sleep. After one walk she returned looking quite pale and with two small puncture marks in her neck. She must have slipped over and fallen on a brooch that I couldn't remember dropping the day before. I decided against mentioning the puncture marks, as Lucy's mother is so ill she is liable to die at any moment. Not that Lucy knows about her mother. In other news, Mr Swales has dropped down dead.

Letter, Mina Harker to Lucy Westenra

24 August: Joyous news. Jonathan was found alive and well and I travelled to meet him in Buda-Pesth where we immediately got wed. He has had a strange time at the castle of Count Dracula and knows not whether the events that passed were real or came to him in a dream. In any case, I have written it all down so I dare say we will all make sense of it sooner or later.

Journal of Lucy Westenra
24 August: I have still not been sleeping well since I returned to London. Last night a bat tried to get in through the window.

Letter, Arthur Holmwood to Dr Seward
31 August: I am very worried about Lucy. Please come urgently to look after her. I have to go and see my father who is dying.

Dr Seward's Diary (kept in phonograph)
2–6 September: If it isn't one thing, it's another. First Renfield is more disturbed than usual and tries to bite me and then Lucy takes another turn for the worse. I send a telegram to Dr Van Helsing, asking him to come urgently from Amsterdam to attend to her. 'Mein Gott,' says the Dutch doctor, bizarrely choosing to talk in German. 'The girl is in a bad way. We must protect her with a bouquet of garlic and flowers and we must give her a blood transfusion.' Arthur arrives back in the nick of time. Luckily, although we didn't know it, Lucy and he are a perfect blood match and the transfusion goes perfectly. For a while Lucy appeared to get better, but then deteriorated rapidly with her breathing becoming most stertorous when her mother removed the garlic as she couldn't stand the smell.

'There is something very strange going on,' said Van Helsing, one afternoon. 'But unfortunately I can't yet tell you what it is or it will spoil the suspense. In the meantime we must do three more blood transfusions as Lucy is perniciously anaemic. I will go first, then Dr Seward and lastly Mr Morris who has conveniently turned up out of nowhere.'

It was with great fortune that all three of us were also perfect blood matches and for a few days Lucy seemed to grow in strength. But then a wolf escaped from London zoo and jumped in through the window, killing Mrs Westenra, and fatally wounding Lucy. Alas, despite our ministrations, she died some days later.

'That's a coincidence,' said Arthur. 'My father also just died; call me Lord Godalming. Can I kiss her goodbye?'

'That wouldn't be a good idea,' Van Helsing replied.

Later that evening, once Arthur had left, Van Helsing explained to me that Lucy was a vampire and must have her head cut off and a stake driven through her heart before she was buried.

'If you'd told us all that earlier, we might have been able to save her,' I said.

Van Helsing apologised, explaining that he hadn't thought that one through.

Journal of Jonathan Harker

23–28 September: A great deal has happened since I last wrote. My employer, Mr Hawkins, has died, making me the new head of the solicitors' firm, and I also thought I saw Count

Dracula wandering around Hyde Park looking a great deal younger than a couple of months ago. Mina has been in touch with Van Helsing, who has summoned us both to London to meet him, Dr Seward and Mr Morris.

'No doubt you have read the newspaper stories of children being abducted on Hampstead Heath and later found with puncture marks on their necks,' Van Helsing began. 'That was Lucy.'

'I thought you said you were going to cut off her head and shove a stake through her body,' said Dr Seward, not unreasonably.

'I forgot,' Van Helsing replied grumpily.

'But aren't there now loads of little kiddies running around London who will grow into vampires?' Seward continued.

'No. Because they haven't had enough blood taken.'

'How do you know? You haven't examined them.'

Van Helsing gave Seward a look of such withering contempt that it brooked no further argument, and suggested we go out to Lucy's grave to complete the grim business. For two nights we waited but were unable to act for reasons that, I must confess, were none too clear to me as on one of the occasions she was lying in her grave with fresh blood dripping from her lips.

But on the third night, as we saved a child from her grasp she did let forth a blood-curdling scream while her eyes turned red.

'It is I, who was to have been her husband, who must do the act,' cried Arthur, thrusting a wooden stake through her heart. Lucy's face did rage with fury, but Arthur was not to be denied. With one cut, he removed her head. 'She is at peace now,' he declared. And, in truth, she was, for her expression did once more resemble the one we all had known in happier times.

Dr Seward's Diary (kept in phonograph)

29 September–4 October: Together we have managed to track down all 50 of the wooden coffins and sterilised them by placing a Holy Host in each. All save one: that which Dracula keeps about his person. 'Till we have found this last one, the world can ne'er be safe from the Undead,' said Van Helsing.

It was while we were looking for the wooden coffins that I realised that the house that Dracula had bought in Purfleet was right next door to my lunatic asylum. Perhaps this, then, explained the strange behaviour of Renfield!

'I do declare that Renfield did always behave with great decency to me on the one occasion I met him,' said Mina. Just then there was a commotion. Renfield was in his cell, his back broken and his head stove in. He groaned piteously, before dying. We rushed back to my office to find Dracula plunging his teeth into Mina and forcing her to drink copiously of his blood. Hard as Morris tried to kill the evil Count, he was unable to prevent him escaping from England.

Mina Harker's Journal

5 October–4 November: It is now incumbent on me to record the next part of this adventure. 'We must follow him even unto the jaws of hell,' said Van Helsing.

'Why?' said I. 'Surely now he is gone I have nothing left to fear?'

'Because he can live for centuries and you are but mortal woman. Time is now to be dreaded, since once he put that mark on your throat.'

'Then how come all the kiddies that Lucy bit aren't in great peril?'

Van Helsing made no answer, leaving me to assume there must be degrees of severity of vampire bite. Truly vampirology is most confusing, for 'tis hard to distinguish between someone being fully Undead or just a little bit Undead and hence able to be made once more alive.

'Let me try to help you,' Van Helsing said, placing a Holy Host on my forehead. I felt a rush of burning pain and my breathing became more stertorous. And yet more stertorous. And more stertorous still.

'Perhaps it would be better if I tried to be of help to you,' I said, glancing in the mirror at the ugly scar that had formed on my head. 'For if I am now under Dracula's command, perhaps I can lead you to him if you hypnotise me at sunrise and sunset when I am least Undead.'

'Truly you have a man-sized brain,' Van Helsing replied. 'Let me put you under.'

'He is going to Varna. No, wait. It's Galatz after all. Actually ...'

Dr Seward's Diary (kept in phonograph)
4 November: Van Helsing and I exchanged worried looks. It was possible Mina was more of a vampire than we had thought and not even her man-sized brain was powerful enough to

fight Dracula's control. 'We must no longer tell her anything in case she were to relay our movements back to the Count,' said Van Helsing. 'It is clear he is headed for his castle.'

Mina Harker's Journal

9 November: All is well. We made it to Dracula's castle where Jonathan and Van Helsing managed to put wafers in the three sisters' coffins while Morris blazed away with his Winchester, before killing the Count with a bowie knife, rendering his body into naught but dust. Sadly Morris died of the wounds that were inflicted on him in the battle. But never mind, I'm feeling a lot better as my scar healed immediately.

Note from Jonathan Harker

Seven year later: Jonathan and I have a son called Quincey. Arthur and Jack are both married and everyone has quite forgotten Lucy. Though, if truth be known, she never appeared to be much remembered while she was alive. Anyway, no more vampires have turned up so far. Touch wood!

ALSO AVAILABLE

Is Heathcliff a Murderer?

In this new edition of his bestselling classic, literary sleuth John Sutherland regales fans of nineteenth-century fiction with the anomalies and conundrums that have emerged from his years of close reading and good-natured pedantry.

Is Oliver Twist dreaming? Why does Dracula come to England? Does Becky kill Jos in *Vanity Fair*? How does Frankenstein make his monsters? And, of course: is Heathcliff really a murderer?

ISBN: 9781785782992 (paperback) / 9781785783005 (ebook)

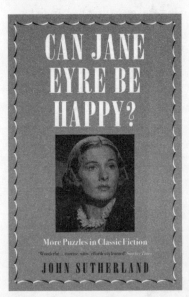

Can Jane Eyre be Happy?

In this follow-up to the enormously successful *Is Heathcliff a Murderer?*, John Sutherland plays literary detective and investigates tantalising conundrums from Daniel Defoe to Virginia Woolf.

How does Magwitch swim to shore with a 'great iron' on his leg? Where does Fanny Hill keep her contraceptives? Does Clarissa Dalloway have an invisible taxi? And, of course: can Jane Eyre really be happy?

ISBN: 9781785783012 (paperback) / 9781785783029 (ebook)